Kierkegaard's

THE CONCEPT OF DREAD

Kierkegaard's

THE CONCEPT OF DREAD

TRANSLATED
WITH INTRODUCTION AND NOTES

BY WALTER LOWRIE

founder upon?

Cnypulwie:

117-18 Mephistopheles: Phenomenology of the "sudden" of dread on suddenly + saying "there"

"the moment reality is posited, possibility steps aside as a nothing which serves as a temptation for all men devoid of thought." 45

PRINCETON
PRINCETON UNIVERSITY PRESS

Copyright 1944, 1957, by Princeton University Press

L.C. Card No. 57-13241

ISBN 0-691-01951-7

SECOND EDITION 1957

First Princeton Paperback Printing, 1967

Fourth Printing, 1973

Printed in the United States of America
by Princeton University Press, Princeton, New Jersey

TRANSLATOR'S PREFACE

THIS being one of the first books S. K. wrote, why is it published so near the end in the English edition? This question has been asked frequently, and lately it has been addressed to me almost petulantly—as though I were responsible! Recently, because many are trying to understand S. K.'s thought as a whole, and in theological seminaries, which in wartime are the last resort of higher learning, courses on S. K. are given wherever any lecturer can be found, this question is being asked more persistently, because the lack of this book is keenly felt. But surely most people will reflect that nobody is culpably responsible for this omission, seeing that the English edition was not planned but simply grew. It is remarkable that it has grown so fast that in the space of eight years thirty of S.K.'s books, besides Dru's big volume of selections from the Journal, have been published in English—at a rate which exceeds the capacity of the public to assimilate them. Yet seeing that this work has been accomplished by ten translators, it is not nearly so remarkable as the fact that all of these works, and as much more again in the way of journals, unfinished writings, etc., were published by S. K. in the space of only ten years—poured out upon the Danish public at a rate which would have produced mental indigestion, if anyone had seriously tried to digest them. It was true also that the original order of publication was not planned. The works simply welled forth as from an inexhaustible spring. Between the *Philosophical Tidbits and a Bit of Philosophy Too* (Swenson called the book *Fragments*, and I owe this name to the Reverend William M. Weber, who invented it when he was a student in Germany) and the *Concluding Unscientific Postscript to the Philosophical Tidbits*, the big book which the little book had promised as its sequel, there intervened nearly two years during which five other books were published. *Tidbits* (as I am fain to call this book ever since I heard the name proposed, which is evidently better than "Scraps," which I first used, not to speak of "Fragments" and "Morsels," and better than "Crumbs," even though I suspect that S. K. may have been thinking of "the crumbs which fell from the rich man's table")—*Tidbits*, or whatever you would call it, was published on June 13, 1844. *Two Edifying Discourses* had been published only five days earlier, *The Concept of Dread* was published on June 17, and on the same day appeared the book called *Prefaces*, which will not likely be translated into English. Thus in one month, indeed in the space of ten days, S. K. issued four books of the most various character: the first was purely religious, the second gave in a nutshell his philosophical position, the third, that is, *The Concept of Dread*, was rightly called psychological, and the fourth S. K. properly described as "light reading," for it was almost purely humorous.

There was, however, a good deal more planning for the English edition than the human understanding is capable of perceiving without revelation. What was lacking was cooperation. How much futile planning there was is attested by the voluminous correspondence I maintained with Professor Swenson on the one hand and with Mr. Dru on the other. Mr. Dru began earlier than I to agitate for the publication of S. K.'s works in English. The first of the many instructive and entertaining letters I received from him was of December 1934, and in that he proposed that the *Stages* (or else *Either/Or*) be published first, and immediately after that *The Concept of Dread* and *The Sickness unto Death*. Early the following year he began to translate *The Concept of Dread*, and that has ever since been regarded as his task. That same year he and Mr. Charles William (on behalf of the Oxford Press) proposed that Dru's translation of that book and my translation of *The Sickness unto Death* might be published at the same time, in September 1939. It would have been very appropriate to publish on the same date the two books which S. K. described as psychological. S. K., however, recognized that with them belonged *Fear and Trembling*, forming a trilogy: Fear, Dread, Despair. He said in the *Postscript* (p. 240, where I do not follow Swenson's translation), "As *Fear and Trembling* was the state of the man teleologically suspended when God tried him, so is Dread the psychic state of the suspended man in that desperate moment of exemption from realizing the ethical." Alas, although my translation of *The Sickness unto Death* was held back for nearly two years, *The Concept of Dread* was not ready to accompany it. Then came the war. At the very beginning of it Mr. Dru was wounded, but he recovered, and now he is employed in the armed forces. In this situation, being unable himself to pursue the work he had begun so zealously, he magnanimously yielded to me the task of translating this book. Upon receipt of his friendly letter I set to work at once to meet the growing demand for this missing link in the

English publication of S. K.'s works, and I labored so diligently that in one month I finished the job—in a month of thirty-one days, working twelve hours a day. There really was no need of putting on so much steam, and it was perhaps petulance at the long delay which prompted me to make this tour de force; for the printing presses in wartime cannot keep pace with such speed. I cannot hope to see this book published before next spring; for the two volumes of *Either/Or* were given to the Press seven months ago, and I do not know when they will be printed. Lately I finished the translation of a big book, S. K.'s *Attack upon "Christendom,"* but rather than hold up *The Concept of Dread*, I prefer to run the risk that the bigger book may not be published before next summer.

It may be judged how important is *The Concept of Dread* from the fact that besides the German translation there are two translations in French and one in Spanish. It is the first time I have had the pleasure of comparing four translations with the original text. It is hard on the eyes to keep five texts in view when I am making my translation, but it is interesting. I soon discovered to my chagrin that the Spanish translation was made, not from the Danish, but from Schrempf's translation, and therefore could be discarded. The translator had not emulated the noble example of Don Miguel de Unamuno, who said in one of his essays, "I learned the language for the sake of reading Ibsen and was rewarded by reading Kierkegaard." Because this translator was only a hack hired by the publisher, his name is not given. But of the French translations,* which were both published in 1935 and are therefore entirely independent, it would be churlish of me to say that they are not very good, seeing that I have profited much by both of them. They were the more useful to me because in eight cases out of ten, even when they discovered the same meaning in the passage, they chose different words to express it. How rich is the French language! A German translation, though it were perfect, would not have helped me so much; for what the English translator seeks and often has to grope after, is the equivalent word in the rich Romance treasury of our language. Professor Ferlov is a Dane. I met him in Rome, where he is an instructor in the University. Such a combination, it seemed to me, must be ideal: a

* *Le Concept d'Angoisse*, by P.-H. Tisseau; *Le Concept de l'Angoisse*, by Knud Ferlov and Jean J. Gateau.

Dane to insure that the Danish is correctly understood, and a Frenchman to put the thing into perfect French. I tried this sort of teamwork, but, alas, it was not a success. To understand Kierkegaard it is not enough to know the Danish language. And in this instance I prefer the work of M. Tisseau, although he did not always understand so well the more colloquial expressions.

This constant comparison impressed upon me the sorrowful thought that at its best the translation of a great writer can hardly be much better than a profanation, a fact which in the Italian language seems axiomatic when it is said, *Traduttore— traditore*. Of course I am thinking principally of my own work as a translator. One of the last letters I had from Dru contained this challenging sentence: "As for Kierkegaard, I am at this moment going through the proofs of our translations. It is a question whether I dislike you or myself most while reading them, and I usually settle it by answering that more than either I loathe Kierkegaard. One of these days I am going to say what I think of his vile, slovenly style, his clumsy, unnecessary terminology."

I was shocked by this impiety. But it is true after all that S. K. was not always a good writer, and now that I have finished the last translation that needs to be done, I am inclined to relieve my feeling in the same way. I have resolved before, "This shall be the last," and have not kept that resolution. This time I shall be faithful to it for the same reason that Adam was faithful to Eve... because there was no other. But I would vent my spite first of all upon the Danish language. S. K. praised his mother tongue in noble terms, and he is said to have done more than anyone else to improve it. He strove to make it better by making it bigger, by introducing innumerable German words and many French ones, so that one needs to have three dictionaries to read him, since the Danish lexicographers have excluded his inventions. As Dru says, his terminology is often maddening. He renounced Hegel, but used his terminology. That we can manage to understand. But, alas, no one can make out what he meant by *bestemt, Bestemmelse*, etc. Swenson once asked me anxiously if I had found any way of dealing with them. I sadly shook my head, and he looked in my eyes with silent despair. I have acquired such a dread of these words, any one of which may mean a dozen things, that when my eye glances furtively down the page and foresees that one of them is coming, I am disposed to close the book and give the whole thing up, or, in the words of Uncle Toby, "I wish I were asleep." *Forhold* is another terrifying word. And why, oh, why did he use so often the words which I have to translate by "constantly" and "precisely"? I beg the reader not to believe that the bad style is always my fault. I express no moral condemnation of punning when I say that the frequent plays on words which S. K. often makes instructive are a great tribulation to the translator, hurdles which he cannot always clear. Since S. K. knew that he "would be studied and studied," knew doubtless that he would be translated into all the greater languages, surely he might have done a little something to make the task of the translator a bit easier.

Having now translated in whole or in part twenty-three of S. K.'s books, I have the impression that this is the most tormenting of them all. It seems to me also that this book shows the greatest unevenness of style. Sudden transitions of style are everywhere observable in S. K.'s works, and it is likely they reflect the changes of mood in a man who was characterized by blended "mania" and depression; but here the situation is not exactly that, here there are no purple patches, no sublime heights attained, the poet is not in evidence; but he does dive to great depths, and then for long stretches moves pedestrianly. In the *Postscript* (p. 240) S. K. himself says about this book that *"The Concept of Dread* is unlike the other pseudonymous works for the fact that its form is direct and even a little like lecturing" (Swenson translates it as "objective dogmatic," which would be well enough except that it does not suggest the contempt which S. K. felt for everything that savors of the docent or the professor).

On the other hand, I cannot ignore the fact that the English language is not always rich enough to render adequately the Danish words. I have mentioned in a note the tribulations everybody has encountered in the effort to translate *Indesluttedhed*. Both Dru and Swenson opened their hearts to me about their troubles with this word. Also, we have no word in our language ambiguous enough to render *aufgehoben,* which Hegel used so adroitly, and for which unfortunately S. K. found a precise equivalent in his mother tongue. It was convenient also for S. K. that in Danish the same word means "sensuous" and "sensual." The reader must keep this in mind. But the very title of this book reveals a serious lack in our language: we have no word which adequately translates *Angst.* In the first translations of fragments of

S. K. published by Professor Hollander in 1924 he used the word "dread," and everyone has agreed to continue it—after a desperate search for something better. The Spanish translation uses *angustia*; Unamuno, writing in French, spoke of *agonie*; it has been seen that both the French translators use *angoisse*. These words rightly indicate the distress of the moment, but do not suggest what is essential to the experience S. K. deals with, that it is an apprehension of the future, a presentiment of a something which is "nothing," that (as he says in the *Christian Discourses*, p. 80) it is "the next day," and, in another place, "it is fighting against the future," therefore against oneself—"and no man is stronger than himself."

Because this book was, as he says, his first effort at "direct" communication, S. K. did not at first propose to use a pseudonym: the title-page as he first devised it (*Papers* V B 42) was to bear his name as the author. Perhaps because it contained so intimate a confession of his "stern upbringing from innate dread to faith" X^2 B 493) he hid behind the name of Vigilius Haufniensis (the Watchman of Copenhagen), and because the preface he originally planned for it (now No. VII in the book called *Prefaces*) was not appropriate to Vigilius he invented a new one to suit him.

And yet this book was not anonymous in the strictest sense, for it was dedicated to Poul Møller in terms which indicate clearly enough a personal affection, even when the stronger terms he at first intended to use were discarded, as I have noted in my *Kierkegaard*, pp. 143 f.

We need not therefore apply to this book S. K.'s emphatic admonition not to attribute to him anything that is said by his pseudonyms. This was his first completely serious book, and everything we find in it may safely be regarded as his own way of thinking.

If I had not worked at such a furious speed, the Reverend Howard Johnson, who did me the favor of correcting the manuscript, might not perhaps have found so many errors; but all's well that ends well, and I am glad to be beholden to him.

Princeton   W A L T E R   L O W R I E
May 26, 1943

INTRODUCTION BY THE TRANSLATOR

THE reader will see at once that this book, in spite of its insistence that every science should be treated by itself, is by no means confined to the science of psychology. The long introduction deals with methodology and metaphysics. Here S. K.'s metaphysical position is stated only negatively, in opposition to Hegel and every school of Idealistic Philosophy. This was the first opportunity he found to deliver a broadside against the Hegelianism which was introduced into Denmark by Heiberg and Martensen. His positive position had already been suggested in the *Fragments* (or *Tidbits*). This metaphysical polemic is by no means unimportant, but we are hardly prepared for it by the title.

There is also in the first chapter more dogmatics than we might expect in a deliberation which proposes to lead us only to the borders of that science. Also there is more mythology than some of us (myself among them) may hanker after. For although S. K. denounced the disposition to treat the story of Adam and Eve as a myth, he nevertheless treats it pretty much as if it were, and is quite frank in rejecting at least the story of the serpent. There is too much about Adam for my taste, and perhaps too much about original sin, although it is very interesting that S. K. is the only modern man who has so profound a sense of the solidarity of the race that original sin makes any sense to him. I have remarked in my preface that there are arid passages in this book which are characterized by abstruse and oversubtle reasoning.

For all that, it was reasonable to describe this book on the title page as "a psychological deliberation," and in this is to be found its unique value. This work and *The Sickness unto Death*, the only books expressly described as psychological, though by no means the only ones in which this interest is prominent, are sufficient in themselves to insure to S. K. a prominent and peculiar place among psychologists. A very peculiar place indeed, for in his time, and still more in ours, even when it does not decline to admit that there is such a thing as a psyche, psychology has been content to remain so much on the surface that there is not much to distinguish it from histology, and even the so-called "deep psychology" of Freud and Jung and Adler does not delve deep enough to discover soul. S. K., because he was intent upon psychoanalyzing himself, his own ego, could not well forget that he was dealing with a soul, a synthesis of soul and body; and because spirit is not obviously and inevitably present in this synthesis, he was compelled (in the best sense of the word) to revert to the Greek and New Testament trichotomy: body, soul, and spirit.

It will not do to dispose of S. K.'s psychology by remarking that his own soul, the soul he chiefly studied, was a sick soul. For not only could he reply that all souls are sick, and that the notion that one has a "healthy-minded" soul is the most perilous of all sicknesses; but all pathologists will agree with him that the study of abnormal states is essential for the understanding of normal health. If it is true that few men have had so sick a soul to deal with as had S. K., and also that no one of them has ever probed so deeply into his sick soul, with such intellectual competence, we may reasonably expect to learn something from his psychology.

Although this book was written, like all of S. K.'s works, in a brief space of time, and, as I remarked in my preface, was published in conjunction with several books which are completely heterogeneous, it must not be supposed that it was hastily thought out. On the contrary, S. K. began early to follow the Delphic (or Socratic) maxim: Know thyself. This appears in the first long entry in his Journal (I A 75; Dru No. 22), and already he was aware of a dread of the good which was nevertheless a fascination, like the fascination which draws the moth to the flame. He developed this thought clearly two years before this book was written (III A 233; Dru No. 402): "People have often explained the nature of original sin, and yet they lacked a primary category— dread, which really is its determinant. For dread is a desire for what one dreads, a sympathetic antipathy. Dread is an alien power which lays hold of an individual, and yet one cannot tear oneself away, nor has a will to do so; for one fears, but what one fears one desires. Dread then makes the individual impotent, and the first sin always occurs in impotence. Apparently, therefore, the man lacks accountability, but this lack is what ensnares him."

Anyone who knows anything about S. K.—even if it is only so much as may be learned from my big and my little biographies— will recognize that his case is described in many of the examples which are adduced as psychological experiments. He suffered from dread of the good as well as from dread of evil (who can entirely disclaim that experience!), and when he says that "the first sin is always committed in impotence" he was mindful of his own case. He wrote in his Journal on May 17, 1843 (IV A 107, p. 43; Dru No. 44, p. 122), "After all, it was dread which caused me to go astray, and where might I seek support when I knew or suspected that the only man I had admired for his strength and power was wavering?"

From the comment upon the pseudonyms which Johannes Climacus is permitted to make in the *Postscript* (pp. 239 f.) we do not get as much enlightenment as we could wish about *The Concept of Dread*. I need refer only to the remark that in view of the futile efforts that have been made to understand sin abstractly, "it is well that it is treated here psychologically." This means that at least a concrete place is assigned to it, for Vigilius rightly insists that sin cannot be understood psychologically.

Because S. K. has furnished us with so little comment upon this book, either in his subsequent works or in his Journal, upon which I am accustomed to draw for my introductions, this introduction may end here. The *Edifying Discourses* often shed light upon the books which they "accompany," but this is the only pseudonymous work (with exception of the serious works of Anti-Climacus) which had no such accompaniment. It was itself so serious that S. K. thought it appropriate to accompany it with the humorous book which he called *Prefaces*, a book which will not likely be translated into English, for the reason only that it dealt with ephemeral interests in the little world of Copenhagen.

THE CONCEPT OF DREAD

A simple psychological deliberation oriented in the
direction of the dogmatic problem
of original sin

BY
VIGILIUS HAUFNIENSIS

Copenhagen
To be had from the University Bookseller
C. A. Reitzel

Printed by Bianco Luno's Press
1844
[June 17.]

The age of distinctions is past and gone, the System has overcome it. He who in our **age** loves distinctions is an eccentric man whose soul clings to that which has long vanished. That may be so, and yet *Socrates* remains what he was, the simple wise man with the curious distinction which he himself expressed by word and by his life, which after full two thousand years the eccentric *Hamann* reiterated, exclaiming with admiration, "Socrates was great for the fact that he 'distinguished between what he understood and what he did not understand.'"

PREFACE

ACCORDING to my notion, he who would write a book does well to think a good deal about the subject on which he would write. Neither would he do ill to form acquaintance, so far as possible, with what has previously been written on the same subject. If along that road he should encounter an individual who has dealt exhaustively and adequately with one or another part of the subject, he does well to rejoice as does the friend of the bridegroom when he stands and gives ear to the bridegroom's voice. When he has done that in perfect silence and with the enthusiasm of a lover, which always seeks solitude, then no more is needed—then he writes his book straightway as the bird sings its ditty, if there be one who profits by it and finds joy in it, so much the better; then he publishes it, carefree and unconcerned, without any self-importance, as though he had said the last word, or as though by his book all generations would be blessed. Every generation has its task and need not disturb itself overmuch to be everything for the preceding and the following generations. Every individual in each generation has likewise every day his own troubles and enough to do in taking care of himself, and does not need to embrace all the contemporary world with sovereign and parental concern, nor to make an era or an epoch[1] begin with his book, still less with the New Year's torch of his vow,[2] or with the far-seeing promises of his suggestive hints, or by reassuring indications with regard to a currency of doubtful value. Not everyone who is round-shouldered is therefore an Atlas or has become so by carrying a world; not everyone who says, "Lord, Lord," enters into the kingdom of heaven; not everyone who offers to go bond for the whole contemporary generation has thereby proved that he is able to vouch for himself; not everyone who cries "Bravo!" "*Schwere Noth!*" "*Gottsblitz!*" "*Bravissimo!*" has therefore understood himself in his admiration.

So far as concerns my humble person, I admit with all honesty that as an author I am a king without a country, but also that in fear and much trembling I am an author without pretensions. If to a noble envy, a jealous criticism, it seems too much that I bear a Latin name, I shall gladly assume the name of John Brown, preferring as I do to be regarded as a layman, one who speculates, it is true, but stands nevertheless far removed from Speculation, even though I am as much a devotee in my faith in authority as the Roman was tolerant in his fear of the gods. As for human authority, I am a fetish-worshiper and with equal piety adore whosoever it may be, if only it is adequately announced betimes by the beating of drums that it is to him I must pay adoration, that he is the Authority and the *Imprimatur*[3] for the current year. It is beyond my understanding how the decision is made, whether this choice comes about by the casting of lots and ballots, or whether the dignity is passed around and the individual sits by turn as an authority just as does a citizen-representative in the Commission of Conciliation.[4]

I have nothing further to add, except that to everyone who shares my view, as also to everyone who does not, to everyone who reads the book, as also to everyone who has enough in the Preface, I would wish a sincere *Lebewohl*!

Respectfully,
VIGILIUS HAUFNIENSIS[5]

CONTENTS

INTRODUCTION

In what sense the subject of this deliberation is a theme of interest to psychology, and in what sense, after having interested psychology, it points precisely to dogmatics.

THE notion that every scientific problem within the great field embraced by science has its definite place, its measure and its bounds, and precisely thereby has its resonance in the whole, its legitimate consonance in what the whole expresses—this notion, I say, is not merely a *pium desiderium* which ennobles the man of science by the visionary enthusiasm or melancholy which it begets, is not merely a sacred duty which employs him in the service of the whole, bidding him renounce lawlessness and the romantic lust to lose sight of land, but it is also in the interest of every more highly specialized deliberation, which by forgetting where its home properly is, forgets at the same time itself (a thought which the very language I use with its striking ambiguity expresses), becomes another thing, and attains a dubious perfectibility by being able to become anything at all. By thus failing to let the scientific call to order be heard, by not being vigilant to forbid the individual problems to hurry by one another as though it were a question of arriving first at the masquerade, one may indeed attain sometimes an appearance of brilliancy, may give sometimes the impression of having already comprehended, when in fact one is far from it, may sometimes by the use of vague words strike up an agreement between things that differ. This gain, however, avenges itself subsequently, like all unlawful acquisitions, which neither in civic life nor in the field of science can really be owned.

Thus when a person entitles the last section of his Logic "Reality,"[1] he thereby gains the advantage of appearing to have already reached by logic the highest thing, or, if one prefers to say so, the lowest. The loss is obvious nevertheless, for this is not to the advantage either of logic or of reality. Not to that of reality, for the contingent, which is an integral part of reality, cannot be permitted to slip into logic. It is not to the advantage of logic, for if logic has conceived the thought of reality it has taken into its system something it cannot assimilate, it has anticipated what it ought merely to predispose. The punishment is clear: that every deliberation about what reality is must by this be made difficult, yea, perhaps for a long time impossible, because this word "reality" will, as it were, require some time to recall to mind what it is, must have time to forget the mistake.

Thus when in dogmatics a person says that *faith* is the *immediate*,[2] without more precise definition, he gains the advantage of convincing everyone of the necessity of not stopping at faith, yea, he compels even the orthodox man to make this concession, because this man perhaps does not at once penetrate the misunderstanding and perceive that it is not due to a subsequent flaw in the argument but to this πρῶτον ψεῦδος. The loss is indubitable, for thereby faith loses by being deprived of what legitimately belongs to it: its historical presupposition. Dogmatics loses for the fact that it has to begin, not where it properly has its beginning, within the compass of an earlier beginning. Instead of presupposing an earlier beginning, it ignores this and begins straightway as if it were logic[3]; for logic in fact begins with the most volatile essence produced by the finest abstraction: the immediate. What then logically is correct, namely, that the immediate is *eo ipso* annulled, becomes twaddle in dogmatics; for to no one could it occur to want to stop with the immediate (not further defined), seeing that in fact it is annulled the instant it is mentioned, just as a sleepwalker awakes the instant his name is called.

Thus when sometimes in the course of investigations which are hardly more than propaedeutic[4] one finds the word "reconciliation" used to designate speculative knowledge, or the identity of the knowing subject and the thing known, the subjective-objective, etc., then one easily sees that the author is brilliant and that by the aid of his *esprit* he has explained all riddles, especially for those who do not even scientifically take the precaution, which yet one takes in everyday life, to listen carefully to the words of the riddle before guessing it. Otherwise one acquires the incomparable merit of having by one's explanation propounded a new riddle, namely, how it could occur to any man that this might be the explanation. That thought possesses reality was the assumption of all ancient philosophy as well as of the philosophy of the Middle Ages. With Kant this assumption became doubtful. Suppose now that the Hegelian school had really *thought through* Kant's scepticism (however, this ought always to remain a big question, in spite of all Hegel and his school[5] have done, by the help of the catchwords

"Method and Manifestation," to hide what Schelling[6] recognized more openly by the cue "intellectual intuition and construction," the fact, namely, that this was a new point of departure) and then reconstructed the earlier view in a higher form, in such wise that thought does not possess reality by virtue of a presupposition— is then this consciously produced reality of thought a reconciliation? In fact philosophy is merely brought back to the point where in old days one began, in the old days when precisely the word "reconciliation" had immense significance. We have an old and respectable philosophical terminology: thesis, antithesis, synthesis. They invent a newer one in which mediation occupies the third place. Is this to be considered such an extraordinary step in advance? Mediation is equivocal, for it designates at once the relation between the two terms and the result of the relation, that in which they stand related to one another as having been brought into relationship; it designates movement, but at the same time rest. Whether this is a perfection, only a far deeper dialectical test will decide; but for that unfortunately we are still waiting. They do away with synthesis and say "mediation." All right. But *esprit* requires more—so they say "reconciliation." What is the consequence? It is of no advantage to their propaedeutic investigations, for of course they gain as little as truth thereby gains in clarity, or as a man's soul increases in blessedness by acquiring a title. On the contrary, they have fundamentally confounded two sciences, ethics and dogmatics—especially in view of the fact that, having got the word "reconciliation" introduced, they now hint that logic is properly the doctrine about the λόγος.[7] Ethics and dogmatics contend in a fateful *confinium* about reconciliation. Repentance and guilt torture out reconciliation ethically, whereas dogmatics in its receptivity for the proffered reconciliation has the historically concrete immediateness with which it begins its discourse in the great conversation of science. What then will be the consequence? That language will presumably have to celebrate a great sabbatical year in which we let speech and thought rest, in order to be able to begin with the beginning.

In logic they use *the negative* as the motive power which brings movement into everything. And movement in logic they must have, any way they can get it, by fair means or foul. The negative helps them, and if the negative cannot, then quibbles and phrases

can, just as the negative itself has become a play on words.* In logic no movement can *come about*, for logic *is*, and everything logical
simply is,† and this impotence of logic is the transition to the
sphere of becoming where existence and reality appear. So when
logic is absorbed in the concretion of the categories it is constantly
the same that it was from the beginning. In logic every movement
(if for an instant one would use this expression) is an immanent
movement, which in a deeper sense is no movement, as one will
easily convince oneself if one reflects that the very concept of movement is a transcendence which can find no place in logic. The negative then is the immanence of movement, it is the vanishing factor,
the thing that is annulled (*aufgehoben*). If everything comes to
pass in that way, then nothing comes to pass, and the negative
becomes a phantom. But precisely for the sake of getting something to come to pass in logic, the negative becomes something
more, it becomes the producer of the opposition, and not a negation but a counterposition. The negative then is not the muteness
of the immanent movement, it is the "necessary other,"[8] which
doubtless must be very necessary to logic in order to set things
going, but the negative it is not. Leaving logic to go on to ethics,
one encounters here again the negative, which is indefatigably active in the whole Hegelian philosophy. Here too a man discovers
to his amazement that the negative is the evil.[9] Now the confusion
is in full swing; there is no bound to brilliancy, and what Mme.
de Staël-Holstein said of Schelling's philosophy,[10] that it gave a

* *Exempli gratia*: Wesen ist was ist gewesen; ist gewesen is the preterite
tense of "to be," *ergo* Wesen is das aufgehoben being "the being which has been."
This is a logical movement! If in the Hegelian logic (such as it is in itself and
through the contributions of the School) one were to take the trouble to pick
out and make a collection of all the fabulous hobgoblins and kobolds which like
busy swains help the logical movement along, a later age would perhaps be
astonished to discover that witticisms which then will appear superannuated
once played a great role in logic, not as incidental explanations and brilliant
observations, but as masters of movement which made Hegel's logic a miracle
and gave the logical thoughts feet to walk on, without anybody noticing it, since
the long cloak of admiration concealed the performer who trained the animals,
just as Lulu [in a play] comes running without anybody seeing the machinery.
Movement in logic is the meritorious service of Hegel, in comparison with which
it is hardly worth the trouble of mentioning the never-to-be-forgotten merits
which Hegel has, and has disdained in order to run after the uncertain—I mean
the merit of having in manifold ways enriched the categorical definitions and
their arrangement.

† The eternal expression of logic is that which the Eleatic School transferred
by mistake to existence: Nothing comes into existence, everything is.

man *esprit* for his whole life, applies in every respect to the Hegelian philosophy. One sees how illogical movements must be in logic since the negative is the evil, and how unethical they must be in ethics since the evil is the negative. In logic this is too much, in ethics too little; it fits nowhere if it has to fit both places. If ethics has no other transcendence, it is essentially logic; if logic is to have so much transcendence as after all has been left in ethics out of a sense of shame, then it is no longer logic.

What I have expounded is perhaps rather prolix for the place where it stands (in relation to the subject with which it deals it is far from being too long), but it is by no means superfluous, since the particular observations are selected with reference to the subject of this work. The examples are taken from the greater world, but what occurs in the great may be repeated in the lesser, and the misunderstanding remains the same, even if the injurious consequences are less. He who gives himself the airs of writing the System[11] has the great responsibility, but he who writes a monograph can be and ought to be faithful over a little.

The present work has taken as its theme the psychological treatment of "dread," in such a way that it has *in mente* and before its eye the dogma of original sin. It has therefore to take account, although tacitly, of the concept of sin. Sin, however, is not a theme for psychological interest, and it would only be to abandon oneself to the service of a misunderstood cleverness if one were to treat it thus/Sin has its definite place, or rather it has no place, and that is what characterizes it. By treating it in a place other than its own, one distorts it, in that one subjects it to an unessential reflective refraction. Its concept is altered, and at the same time the mood which properly corresponds to the correct concept* is confused, and instead of the endurance of the genuine mood one has the fleeting jugglery of the false mood. Thus when sin is drawn into aesthetics the mood becomes either frivolous or melancholy; for the category under which sin lies is contradiction, and this is either comic or tragic/The mood is therefore falsified,

---

* The fact that science, fully as much as poetry and art, assumes a mood both on the part of the producer and on the part of the recipient, that an error in modulation is just as disturbing as an error in the exposition of thought, has been entirely forgotten in our age, when people have altogether forgotten the nature of inwardness and appropriation in their joy over all the glory they believed they possessed, or through cupidity have lost it, like the dog[12] which preferred the shadow. However, every error begets its own enemy. An error of thought has outside cf it as its enemy, dialectics; the absence of mood or its falsification has outside of it its enemy, the comical.

for the mood corresponding to sin is seriousness. Its concept is altered, for whether it becomes comic or tragic, it is either an enduring thing, or a thing which as unessential is annulled [*aufgehoben*], whereas properly its concept is, to be overcome. In a deeper sense the comical and the tragical have no enemies; the antagonist is either a bogy which makes one weep, or a bogy which makes one laugh.

If sin is dealt with in metaphysics, the mood is the dialectical indifference and disinterestedness which thinks sin through as something which cannot resist thought. The concept is altered; for it is true that sin has to be overcome, not however as that to which thought is unable to give life, but as that which exists and as such is everybody's concern.

If sin is dealt with in psychology, the mood becomes the persistence of observation, the dauntlessness of the spy, not the ardent flight of seriousness away from and out of sin. The concept becomes a different one, for sin becomes a state. But sin is not a state. Its idea is that its concept is constantly annulled. As a state (*de potentia*) it *is* not, whereas *de actu* or *in actu* it is and is again. The mood of psychology would be antipathetic curiosity, but the correct mood is the stouthearted opposition of seriousness. The mood of psychology is the dread corresponding to its discovery, and in its dread it delineates sin, while again and again it is alarmed by the sketch it produces. When sin is treated in such a way it becomes the stronger; for psychology is really related to it in a feminine way. Doubtless there is an element of truth in this state of mind, and doubtless it emerges in every man's life more or less before the ethical makes its appearance; but by such treatment sin becomes not what it is but more or less than it is.

As soon therefore as one sees the problem of sin treated, it is possible at once to see from the mood whether the concept is the right one. For example, as soon as sin is talked about as a sickness, an abnormality, a poison, a disharmony, then the concept too is falsified.

Sin does not properly belong in any science. It is the theme with which the sermon deals, where the individual talks as an individual to the individual. In our age scientific self-importance has turned the priests into professorial parish-clerks of a sort, who also serve science and think it beneath their dignity to preach. It is no wonder therefore that preaching has come to be regarded as a pretty poor art. Nevertheless, preaching is the most difficult of all arts, and essentially it is the art which Socrates[13] extols: the art of being able to converse. From this of course it does not follow that there must be someone in the congregation to make answer, or that it might be a help to have someone regularly introduced to speak. (When Socrates censured the Sophists by making the distinction that they were able to talk but not to converse, what he really meant was that they were able to say a great deal about everything, but lacked the factor of personal appropriation. Appropriation is precisely the secret of conversation.)

To the concept of sin corresponds the mood of seriousness. The science in which sin might most plausibly find a place would surely be ethics. About this, however, there is a great difficulty. Ethics is after all an ideal science, and that not only in the sense that every other science is ideal. Ethics would bring ideality into reality; on the other hand its movement is not designed to raise reality up into ideality.* Ethics points to ideality as a task and assumes that man is in possession of the conditions requisite for performing it. Thereby ethics develops a contradiction, precisely for the fact that it makes the difficulty and the impossibility clear. What is said of the Law[14] applies to ethics, that it is a severe schoolmaster, which in making a demand, by its demand only condemns, does not give birth to life. Only the Greek ethics constituted an exception, due to the fact that it was not ethics in the proper sense but contained an aesthetic factor. This is evinced clearly in its definition of virtue[15] and in what Aristotle says often but also in *Ethica Nicomachea* affirms with charming Greek naïveté that, after all, virtue alone does not make a man happy and content, but he must have health, friends, earthly goods, be happy in his family. The more ideal ethics is, the better. It must not let itself be disturbed by the twaddle that it is no use requiring the impossible; for even to listen to such talk is unethical, is something for which ethics has neither *time* nor *opportunity*. Ethics does not have to chaffer, nor in that way does one reach reality. If that is to be reached, the whole movement must be reversed. This characteristic of ethics, namely, that it is so ideal, is what tempts one in the treatment of it to employ

* If one will consider this more sharply, one will have opportunity to perceive how brilliant it was to entitle the last section of logic "Reality," inasmuch as not even ethics reaches that. The reality with which logic ends signifies therefore in the way of reality no more than that "being" with which it begins.

now a metaphysical category, now an aesthetical, now a psychological. But of course ethics above all sciences must withstand temptations, but because there are these temptations no one can write an ethics without having entirely different categories up his sleeve.

Sin belongs to ethics only in so far as upon this concept it founders by the aid of repentance.* If ethics must include sin,

* With regard to this point one will find several observations by Johannes de silentio, author of *Fear and Trembling* (Copenhagen 1843). There the author several times allows the wishful ideality of the aesthetical to founder upon the exacting ideality of the ethical, in order by these collisions to let the religious ideality come to evidence, which is precisely the ideality of reality, and therefore is just as desirable as that of aesthetics and not impossible like that of ethics, yet to let it come to evidence in such a way that it breaks out in the dialectical leap and with the positive feeling, "Behold, all things have become new!" and in the negative feeling which is the passion of the absurd to which the concept of "repetition" corresponds. Either the whole of existence is locked up in the requirement of ethics, or the condition for its fulfillment must be provided—and with that the whole of life and of existence begins afresh, not through an immanent continuity with the foregoing (which is a contradiction), but by a transcendent fact which separates the repetition from the first existence by such a cleft that it is only a figure of speech to say that the foregoing and the subsequent state are related to one another as the totality of the living creatures in the sea are related to those in the air and on the land, although according to the opinion of some natural scientists the former is supposed to be the prototype which in its imperfection prefigures everything which becomes manifest in the latter. With regard to this category one may compare *Repetition* by Constantine Constantius (Copenhagen 1843). This book is in fact a whimsical book, as its author meant it to be, but nevertheless it is so far as I know the first which has energetically conceived repetition and let it be glimpsed in its pregnance to explain the relation between the ethnical and the Christian, by indicating the invisible summit and the *discrimen rerum* where science breaks against science until the new science comes forth. But what he has discovered he has hidden again by arraying the concept in the form of jest which aptly offers itself as a mode of presentation. What has moved him to do this it is difficult to say, or rather it is difficult to understand; for he says himself that he writes this "so that the heretics might not be able to understand him." As he has only wished to employ himself with this subject aesthetically and psychologically, he had to plan it all humoristically, and the effect is produced by the fact that the word at one moment signifies everything, and the next moment the most insignificant thing, and the transition, or rather the perpetual falling from the stars, is justified as a burlesque contrast. However, he stated the whole thing pretty clearly on page 34: "Repetition is the *interest* of metaphysics and at the same time the interest upon which metaphysics founders. Repetition is the solution in every ethical view; repetition is a *conditio sine qua non* of every dogmatic problem." The first sentence contains an allusion to the thesis that metaphysics is disinterested, as Kant[16] affirmed of aesthetics. As soon as the interest emerges, metaphysics steps to one side. For this reason the word interest is italicized. The whole interest of subjectivity emerges in real life, and then metaphysics founders. In case repetition is not posited, ethics remains a binding power; presumably it is for this reason he says that "it is the solution in every ethical view." If repetition is not posited, dogmatics cannot exist at all; for in faith repetition be-

its ideality is lost. The more it remains in its ideality, and yet never becomes inhuman enough to lose sight of reality, but corresponds with this by willing to suggest itself as a task for every man, in such a way as to make him the true man, the whole man, the man κατ' ἐξοχήν, all the greater is the tension of the difficulty it proposes. In the fight to realize the task of ethics sin shows itself not as something which only casually belongs to a casual individual, but sin withdraws deeper and deeper as a deeper and deeper presupposition, as a presupposition which goes well beyond the individual. Now all is lost for ethics, and ethics has contributed to the loss of all. There has come to the fore a category which lies entirely outside its province. *Original sin* makes everything still more desperate—that is to say, it settles the difficulty, not, however, by the help of ethics but by the help of *dogmatics*. As all ancient thought and speculation were founded upon the assumption that thought had reality, so also all ancient ethics upon the assumption that virtue is realizable. Scepticism of sin is entirely foreign to paganism. For the ethical consciousness, sin is what an error is in relation to knowledge, it is the particular exception which proves nothing.

gins, and faith is the organ for the dogmatic problems.—In the sphere of nature repetition exists in its immovable necessity. In the sphere of spirit the problem is not to get change out of repetition and find oneself comfortable under repetition, as though the spirit stood only in an external relation to the repetitions of the spirit (in consequence of which good and evil alternate like summer and winter), but the problem is to transform repetition into something inward, into the proper task of freedom, into freedom's highest interest, as to whether, while everything changes, it can actually realize repetition. Here the finite spirit falls into despair. This Constantine has indicated by stepping aside and letting repetition break forth in the young man by virtue of the religious. Therefore Constantine says several times that repetition is a religious category, too transcendent for him, that it is a movement by virtue of the absurd, and on page 144 it is said that eternity is the true repetition. All this Professor Heiberg[17] has failed to observe, but he has very kindly wished by his knowledge (which like his New Year's gift-book is singularly elegant and up-to-date) to help this work to become a tasteful and elegant insignificance, by pompously bringing the question back to the point where (to recall a recent book) the aesthetic writer in *Either/Or* had brought it in "The Rotation of Crops." If Constantine were really to feel himself flattered by enjoying in this instance the rare honor which brings him into an undeniably elect company—then to my way of thinking, since it was he who wrote the book, he must have become stark mad. But if on the other hand an author like him, who writes in order to be misunderstood, were so far to forget himself and had not ataraxia enough to account it to his credit that Professor Heiberg had not understood him—then again he must be stark mad. And this I have no need to fear, for the circumstance that hitherto he has not replied to Professor Heiberg indicates that he has adequately understood himself.

With dogmatics begins the science which, in contrast to that science of ethics which can strictly be called ideal, starts with reality. It begins with the real in order to raise it up into the ideality. It does not deny the presence of sin, on the contrary, it assumes it, and explains it by assuming original sin. However, since dogmatics is very seldom treated purely, one will often find original sin drawn into its domain in such a way that the impression of the heterogeneous originality of dogmatics does not strike the eye but is obscured, which happens also when one finds in it a dogma about angels,[18] about the Holy Scripture, etc. Dogmatics therefore should not explain original sin but expound it by assuming it, like that vortex the Greeks[19] talked so much about, a something originating movement, upon which no science can lay its hand.

That such is the case with dogmatics will readily be admitted when one finds leisure to understand for a second time Schleiermacher's immortal services[20] to this science. People long ago deserted him when they chose Hegel, and yet Schleiermacher was in the beautiful Greek sense a thinker who could talk of what he has known, whereas Hegel, in spite of his remarkable and colossal learning, reminds us nevertheless again and again by his performance that he was in the German sense a professor of philosophy on a big scale, who *à tout prix* must explain all things.

The new science then begins with dogmatics, in the same sense that the immanent science begins with metaphysics. Here ethics finds its place again as the science which has the dogmatic consciousness of reality as a task for reality. This ethic does not ignore sin, and its ideality does not consist in making ideal requirements, but its ideality consists in the penetrating consciousness of reality, of the reality of sin, yet not, be it observed, with metaphysical frivolity or psychological concupiscence.

One readily sees the difference of the movement, and that the ethic of which we are now speaking belongs to another order. The first ethic foundered upon the sinfulness of the individual. So far from being able to explain this, the difficulty had to become still greater and ethically more enigmatic, for the fact that the sin of the individual widens out and becomes the sin of the whole race. At this juncture came dogmatics and helped by the doctrine of original sin. The new ethics presupposes dogmatics and along with that original sin, and by this it now explains the sin of the individual, while at the same time it presents ideality as a task, not however by a movement from above down, but from below up.

It is well known that Aristotle[21] used the name πρώτη φιλοσοφία [the first philosophy] and denoted by that more especially metaphysics, although he included also a part of what to our notion belongs to theology. It is entirely natural that in paganism theology should be treated in this place; it evinces the same lack of infinite penetrating reflection which accounts for the fact that in paganism the theater had reality as a sort of divine worship. If now one will waive the objection to this ambiguity, we might retain this name and understand by πρώτη φιλοσοφία* the totality of science, we might describe it as ethnic, the nature of it being immanence, or use the Greek term "recollection"; and understand by *secunda philosophia* that of which the nature is transcendence or "repetition."†

The concept of sin does not properly belong in any science; only the second ethics can deal with its apparition but not with its origin. If any other science were to discuss it, the concept would be confused. For example, coming closer to our theme, if psychology were to do so.

What psychology has to deal with must be something in repose, something which abides in a mobile state of quiet, not with an unquiet thing which constantly reproduces itself or is repressed. But the abiding state, that out of which sin constantly becomes (comes into being), not by necessity, for a becoming by necessity is simply a state of being (as is for example the entire history of the plant), but by freedom—in this abiding state, I say, which is the predisposing assumption, the real possibility of sin, we have a subject for the interest of psychology. That which can concern psychology and with which it can concern itself is the question how sin can come into existence, not the fact that it exists. In its interest in its object psychology carries the thing so far that it is as if sin were there; but the next thing, the fact that it is there,

---

* Schelling[22] recalled this Aristotelian name to favor his distinction between negative and positive philosophy. By negative philosophy he understood "logic," that was clear enough; on the other hand it was not so clear to me what he really understood by "positive," except in so far as it remained indubitable that positive philosophy was that which he himself provided. However, it is not feasible to go into that, since I have nothing to hold on to except my own interpretation.

† Of this Constantine Constantius has reminded us by pointing out that immanence founders upon "interest." It is in fact with this concept that reality first comes into view.

is qualitatively different from this. To show then that this presupposition for the careful observation of psychology turns out to be more and more comprehensive is the interest of psychology; yea, psychology is willing to abandon itself to the illusion that hereby sin is really posited. But this last illusion betrays the impotence of psychology and shows that it has served its turn.

That human nature must be such that it makes sin possible, is, psychologically speaking, perfectly true; but to want to let this possibility of sin become its reality is shocking to ethics and sounds to dogmatics like blasphemy; for freedom is never possible; as soon as it is, it is actual, in the same sense in which it has been said by an earlier philosophy[23] that when God's existence is possible it is necessary.

As soon as sin is really posited, ethics is on the spot and follows every step it takes. How it came into being does not concern ethics, except in so far as it is certain that sin came into the world as sin. But still less than with the genesis of sin is ethics concerned with the still life of its possibility.

If one would ask more particularly in what sense and to what extent psychology pursues the object of its investigation, it is clear from the foregoing and in itself that every observation of the reality of sin as an object of thought is irrelevant to it, nor as the object of observation does it belong to ethics either, for ethics never acts as observer, but accuses, condemns, acts. In the next place, it follows from the foregoing and is evident in itself that psychology has nothing to do with the details of empirical actuality, except in so far as they are outside of sin. As a science, psychology can never have anything to do empirically with the detail which underlies it, and yet this detail may receive its scientific representation in proportion as psychology becomes more and more concrete. In our age this science, which above all others has leave to intoxicate itself, one might almost say, with the foaming multifariousness of life, has become as spare in its diet and as ascetic as any anchorite. This is not the fault of the science but of its devotees. In relation to sin, on the other hand, this whole content of reality is properly denied to it, only the possibility of it still belongs to it. To ethics of course the possibility of sin never presents itself, and ethics never lets itself be fooled into wasting its time upon such reflections. Psychology, on the other hand, loves them; it sits sketching the contours and measuring the angles of possibility, and no more would let itself be disturbed than would Archimedes.[24]

But while psychology thus delves into the possibility of sin, it is without knowing it in the service of another science, which is only waiting for it to be finished in order to begin for its part and help psychology to an explanation. This other science is not ethics, for ethics has nothing whatsoever to do with this possibility. No, it is dogmatics, and here in turn the problem of original sin emerges. While psychology is fathoming the real possibility of sin, dogmatics explains original sin, which is the ideal possibility of sin. On the other hand, the second ethics has nothing to do with the possibility of sin nor with original sin. The first ethics ignores sin, the second ethics has the reality of sin in its province, and here only by a misunderstanding can psychology intrude.

If what has been here expounded is correct, one will easily see with what justification I have called this book a psychological deliberation, and will see also how this deliberation, in so far as it brings to consciousness its relation to science in general, properly belongs to psychology and leads in turn to dogmatics. Psychology has been called the doctrine of the subjective spirit.[25] If one will pursue this science a little more precisely, one will see how, when it comes to the problem of sin, it must change suddenly into the doctrine of the Absolute Spirit. Here is the place of dogmatics. The first ethics presupposes metaphysics, and the second dogmatics; but it also completes it in such a way that here as everywhere the presupposition comes to evidence.

This was the task of the introduction. The introduction may be correct while the deliberation itself dealing with the concept of dread may be entirely incorrect. That remains to be seen.

CHAPTER I

Dread as the presupposition of original sin and as explaining it retrogressively by going back to its origin

§ 1

Historical indications relative to the concept of original sin

Is this concept identical with the concept of the first sin, Adam's sin, the Fall? So it has sometimes been understood, and consequently the task proposed was to explain in an identical way original sin and the sin of Adam. Since thought here stumbles upon difficulties, theologians sought a way out. In order at least to explain something they introduced a fantastic assumption, a state which by its loss involved the Fall. They gained thus the advantage that everybody would be willing to concede that such a state as that described is not found in the world, but they forgot that the doubt was a different one, namely, whether it ever had existed—and that was pretty clearly necessary if one were to lose it. The history of the human race acquires a fantastic beginning, Adam was fantastically put outside, pious sentiment and fantasy got what it desired, a godly prelude, but thought got nothing. In a double way Adam was kept fantastically outside. The assumption was a dialectic-fantastic one, especially in Catholicism (Adam lost *donum divinitus datum supranaturale et admirabile*).[1] It was historically fantastic, especially in the Covenant Theology,[2] which lost itself dramatically in an imaginary notion of Adam acting as plenipotentiary representative of the whole race. Of course both explanations explain nothing, since the one explains away what it had itself poetically interpolated, and the other merely introduced poetry which explains nothing.

Is the concept of original sin so different from the concept of the first sin that the individual participates in it only through his relation to Adam and not through his primordial relation to sin? If so, then Adam is again fantastically placed outside history. Adam's sin is then more than passed (*plus quam perfèctum*). Original sin is present, it is sinfulness, and Adam was the only one in whom this was not, since it came into being by means of him. They were not attempting therefore to explain Adam's sin, but would explain original sin by its consequences. The explanation, however, was not meant for thought. Hence one can understand very well that a symbolical document affirms the impossibility of an explanation, and that this affirmation is made without contradicting the explanation. The Articles of Smalkald teach expressly: *peccatum haereditarium tam profunda et tetra est corruptio naturae, ut nullius hominis ratione intelligi possit, sed ex scripturae patefactione agnoscenda et credenda sit*. This affirmation is perfectly compatible with the explanations; for in them we have not thought-definitions as such, but here pious feelings (in the direction of the ethical) give vent to their indignation at original sin, assume the role of prosecutor, and then, with an almost feminine passion, with the exaltation of a young girl in love, they are solely concerned to make sinfulness more and more odious, oneself included, so that no word is hard enough to denounce the participation of the individual in this sinfulness. If with this in mind one will survey the various confessions, one will discover a gradation in which the profound Protestant piety comes off victorious. The Greek Church calls original sin ἁμάρτημα πρωτοπατορικόν [the sin of the first father]. It has not even a concept, for this term is only a historical statement, which does not like a concept indicate a present condition but only the historically concluded fact. *Vitium originis* [a sin of origin] (Tertullian) is indeed a concept, but nevertheless the form of the language allows one to conceive the historical factor as predominant. *Peccatum originale* (*quia originaliter tradatur*) (Augustine) states the concept, which becomes even more clearly defined by the distinction between *peccatum originans* and *originatum*. Protestantism rejects Scholastic definitions (*carentia imaginis dei, defectus justitiae originalis*), as it does also the notion that sin might be *poena*[3] (*concupiscentiam poenam esse non peccatum, disputant adversarii*, Apol. A.C.) ; and now begins the enthusiastic climax: *vitium, peccatum, reatus, culpa*. One cares only for the eloquence of the contrite soul, and therefore may sometimes let a perfectly contradictory thought slip into the discourse about original sin (*nunc quoque afferens iram dei iis, qui secundum exemplum Adami peccarunt*). Or that troubled eloquence is utterly careless of thought but affirms terrific things about original sin (*quo fit ut omnes propter inobedientiam Adae et Hevae in odio apud deum simus*, says the *Formula Concordiae*, which nevertheless is prudent enough to protest against thinking this, for if one were to think it, sin, as it says, would become man's substance).*

As soon as the exaltation of faith and contrition has vanished one can no longer be helped by such definitions, which only make it easy for cunning common sense to escape the recognition of sin. But to need other definitions is a dubious proof of the perfection of our age, quite in the same sense as is our need of other than Draconian laws.

The same fantastic effect so evident here is repeated again at another point in dogmatics, the Atonement. It is affirmed that Christ made satisfaction for original sin. But how was it then with Adam? He in fact brought original sin into the world. Was not then original sin an actual sin in him? Or does original sin signify the same thing for Adam as for every man in the race? If so, then the concept is annulled. Or was Adam's whole life original sin? Did not the first sin engender in him other sins, i.e. actual sins? The defect in the previous theory is here more evident; for Adam now finds himself so fantastically outside that he is the only one who is excluded from the Atonement. *An the fit men.*

* The fact that the *Form. Conc.* forbade one to think this definition must nevertheless be extolled as a proof of the energetic passion with which it knew how to let thought stumble against the unthinkable, an energy which is very admirable in contrast with modern thought which is only too loosely strung. [I have been told (but too late to add anything to the notes at the end of the volume) that I ought to translate for the unlearned all the phrases in Latin etc. which S. K. uses so frequently. I must tuck in here all that refers to the paragraph preceding this note. The article of Smalkald states that "hereditary sin is so deep and dreadful a corruption of nature that it cannot be understood by the reason of any man but must be recognized and believed by the revelation of Scripture." The phrase ascribed to Augustine (which has not been traced to its source) means, "original sin, so called because it was handed down from the origin of the race"; and the distinction between *pecatum originans* etc. expresses the difference between original sin as productive of subsequent sins, and the sin thus produced. The Protestants are said to reject the notion that "original sin is deprivation of the image of God, a loss of original righteousness," and to deny that "concupiscence is punishment, not sin." What is here called a "climax" is fault, sin, culpability, guilt. *Nunc quoque* means: "now bringing down also God's wrath upon them that sinned after the example of Adam," and *quo fit* etc. means: "wherefore on account of the disobedience of Adam and Eve we are all the objects of God's hate."]

However one may state the problem, as soon as Adam finds himself fantastically outside, everything is confused. To explain Adam's sin is therefore to explain original sin, and no explanation is of any avail which explains original sin and does not explain Adam. The deepest reason for this is to be discovered in the essential characteristic of human existence, that man is an individual and as such is at once himself and the whole race, in such wise that the whole race has part in the individual, and the individual has part in the whole race.* If one does not hold fast to this, one either gets into the singularity of Pelagianism, Socinianism, or philanthropy, or else falls into the fantastic. The prose of common sense is that the race is resolved numerically into a "one times one." The fantastic is that Adam enjoys the well-meant honor of being more than the whole race, or the ambiguous honor of standing outside the race.

The fact is that at every moment the individual is himself and the race. This is man's perfection, regarded as a state. At the same time it is a contradiction; but a contradiction is always the expression for a task; but a task is movement; but a movement towards that same thing as a task which first was given up as an enigma is a historical movement. Hence the individual has a history; but if the individual has a history, so has also the race. Every individual has the same perfection; precisely for this cause the individuals do not fall away from one another numerically, any more than does the concept of the race become a phantom. Every individual is essentially interested in the history of all other individuals, yea, just as essentially as in his own. Perfection in oneself means therefore the perfect participation in the whole. No individual is indifferent to the history of the race, any more than is the race to that of any individual. While the history of the race goes on, the individual regularly begins afresh, because he is himself and the race, and hence in turn his is the history of the race.

Adam is the first man; he is at once himself and the race. It is not by virtue of the aesthetically beautiful that we adhere to him; it is not by virtue of a magnanimous sentiment that we attach

* If an individual could fall away from the race entirely, his falling away would involve a modification of the race, whereas on the contrary, if a beast were to fall away from the species, the species would be entirely unaffected.

ourselves to him, in order not to leave him so to say in the lurch as one who was to blame for everything; it is not by virtue of the enthusiasm of sympathy and the persuasiveness of piety that we resolve to share this guilt with him, as the child wishes to be guilty along with the father; it is not by virtue of a forced compassion which teaches us to put up with what we cannot mend; but it is by virtue of thought we hold fast to him. Therefore every effort to explain Adam's significance for the race as *caput generis humani naturale, seminale, foederale*[4] (to recall the dogmatic expressions), confuses everything. He is not essentially different from the race, for in that case there is no race; he is not the race, for in that case there is no race: he is himself and the race. Therefore what explains Adam explains the race, and vice versa.

§2

The concept of the first sin

ACCORDING to traditional conceptions, the difference between Adam's first sin and the first sin of every man is this: Adam's sin conditions sinfulness as a consequence; the other first sin assumes sinfulness as a condition. If that were so, then Adam would really be outside the race, and the race did not begin with him but had a beginning outside itself, and this runs contrary to every concept.

It is easy to see that the *first* sin signifies something different from a sin (i.e. a sin like several others), something different from one sin (i.e. No. 1 in relation to No. 2). The first sin is a determinant of quality, the first sin is *the* sin. This is the secret of "the first," and the scandal of it for abstract intelligence, which thinks that once is nothing much, but that many times is something, a notion which is altogether preposterous, inasmuch as each of the many times either signifies as much as the first time, or all of them taken together not nearly so much. It is therefore a superstition to affirm in logic that by a continued quantitative progression a new quality is produced; it is an unpardonable reticence when one does not indeed conceal the fact that things do not go on quite in this way but conceals the consequence of this for the whole logical immanence by inserting it in the midst of the logical movement as Hegel does.* The new quality appears with the first, with the leap, with the suddenness of the enigmatic.

If the first sin signifies numerically one sin, then no history results from it, and sin has no history either in the individual or in the race; for the condition for both is the same, even though the history of the race is not for this reason the history of the individual, any more than the history of the individual is that of the race, except in so far as the contradiction constantly expresses the task.

With the first sin came sin into the world. Exactly in the same way is this true of every subsequent first sin of man, that with it sin comes into the world. The fact that it was not there before Adam's first sin is (in relation to sin itself) an altogether accidental and irrelevant reflection which has altogether no significance, and is no justification for making Adam's sin greater or the first sin of every other man less. It is really a logical and ethical heresy to give the impression that sinfulness in a man goes on determining itself quantitatively for so long a time that at last by a *generatio aequivoca* it produces the first sin in man. This does not come to pass. It did not come to pass that Trop,[9] who yet was a master in quantitative determination, got the dégree of candidate in law by the aid of it. Let the mathematicians and astronomers help themselves out if they can with infinitely small magnitudes; in everyday life this does not help one to get one's certificate as candidate, and still less to explain spirit. If the first sin of every subsequent man were to issue in this way out of sinfulness, his first sin is only unessentially defined when we call it "the first," but would be essentially defined by its serial number (if we can think of such a thing) in the general sinking

* After all, this thesis about the relation between the quantitative determination and the new quality has a long history. In effect, the whole Greek sophistic consisted in affirming a quantitative definition, and hence for it the highest expression of diversity is likeness and unlikeness. In modern philosophy Schelling[5] first wanted to help himself out with a merely quantitative determinant to explain all diversity; subsequently he censured this same thing in Eschenmayer[6] (in his doctoral dissertation). Hegel[7] affirmed the leap, but affirmed it in logic. Rosenkrantz (in his *Psychology*) admires Hegel for this. In the latest work of Rosenkrantz[8] that has been published (about Schelling) he censures this and praises Hegel. But Hegel's misfortune is precisely this, that he wants to assert the new quality and yet does not want to, since he wants to do it in logic, which, no sooner than this is recognized, must acquire a different consciousness of itself and of its significance.

fund of the race. But thus it is not, and it is equally foolish, illogical, unethical, un-Christian, to want to sue for the honor of being the first discoverer, and to want to slink away from something by not being willing to think anything by saying that one has not done anything else but what all the others have done. The presence of sinfulness in a man, the power of example, etc., are only quantitative determinants which explain* nothing, unless it is assumed that one individual is the whole race, instead of every individual being himself and the whole race.

The account of the first sin in Genesis has, especially in our age, been regarded rather carelessly as a myth. There is some reason for this, inasmuch as what one put in place of it was indeed a myth, and a poor one at that. For when the understanding takes to mythology there seldom comes out of it anything but twaddle. That account in Genesis is the only dialectically consistent account. Really its whole substance is concentrated in the clause: *Sin came into the world by a sin.* If this were not so, then sin would have come in as something accidental, which man would do well not to try to explain. The difficulty for the understanding is precisely the triumph of the explanation, its profound consistency in representing that sin presupposes itself, that it so came into the world that by the fact that it is, it is presupposed. Sin comes in as the sudden, i.e. with the leap; but this leap posits at the same time the quality; but when the quality was posited, the leap that same instant turned into the quality and was presupposed by the quality, and the quality by the leap. This is a stumbling block to the understanding, *ergo* it is a myth. In requital the understanding composes poetically a myth which denies the leap, construes the circle as a straight line, and then everything goes on as a matter of course. It paints a fantastic picture of *how* man was before the Fall, and gradually, as the understanding chatters about it, the assumed innocence becomes little by little, in the course of the twaddle, sinfulness—and so there it is. The discourse of the understanding in this instance may aptly be compared with the infantile rigmarole in which childhood takes delight: "One nis ball," "two nis balls," "three nis balls," etc., up to "nine nis balls" and "tennis balls"— here it is, and elicited quite naturally by the foregoing. If there

---

* What significance they may have in other regards, as concomitants in the history of the race, as the run preparatory to the leap, which does not, however, explain the leap, is another question.

might be anything in this myth invented by the understanding, it
would be that sinfulness precedes sin. But if this is true in the sense
that sinfulness has come in by any other way but by sin, then the
concept is annulled. But if it has come in by sin, then sin has preceded it. This contradiction is the only dialectically consistent statement, which is able to do justice to both the leap and immanence
(i.e. the subsequent immanence).

So by Adam's sin *sin came into the world*. This statement,
which is the common one, implies however a reflection which is
entirely external, and this doubtless has contributed much to the
rise of the vague misunderstanding. That sin came into the world
is quite true, but this statement as it stands does not concern Adam.
To express the situation quite sharply and accurately one must say
that by the first sin sinfulness came into Adam. It would not
occur to anybody to say of any subsequent man that by his first
sin sinfulness came into the world, and yet it comes through him
in like manner (i.e. in a manner which is not essentially different)
into the world; for, sharply and accurately expressed, sinfulness
is in the world only in so far as it comes in through sin.

The fact that Adam has been interpreted differently is due
solely to the consideration that the consequences of Adam's fantastic relation to the race must be everywhere made evident. His
sin is original sin. Nothing else is known of him. But original sin
as seen in Adam is only that first sin. Is Adam the only individual
who has no history? Then indeed the race has to begin with an
individual who is not an individual, whereby both the concept of
the race and that of the individual are annulled. If any other individual in the race can by his history have significance in the
history of the race, Adam has it, too; if Adam has significance
only by reason of that first sin, then the concept of history is annulled, that is to say, history was finished the same instant it began.*

Owing to the fact that the race does not begin afresh with every

---

* The point is to get Adam back into the human race, exactly in the same
sense in which every other individual is. This the theologians ought to look
after, especially for the sake of the Atonement. The doctrine that Adam and
Christ correspond to one another[10] explains nothing at all, but confuses everything. There may be an analogy, but the analogy is in the concept incomplete.
Only Christ is an individual who is more than an individual; but for this reason
he did not come in the beginning but in the fullness of time.

individual* the sinfulness of the race acquires a history. This however proceeds by quantitative determinants, while the individual by the qualitative leap participates in it. The race therefore does not begin afresh with every individual, for in that way the race would be no race, but every individual begins afresh with the race.

If one would say that Adam's sin brought the sin of the race into the world, one either means this fantastically, and thereby every concept is annulled, or one can with the same justification say it of every man who by his first sin brings in sinfulness. Getting an individual who has to stand outside the race to begin the race is a myth of the understanding, like that of letting sinfulness begin in any other way but by sin. What one attains is merely to retard the problem, which naturally turns then to man No. 2 for an explanation, or rather now it is man No. 1, since the first man No. 1 has become in effect No. 0.

What often deludes people and helps to start all sorts of fantastic notions going is the fact of generation, as if the subsequent man were essentially different from the first because he is a descendant. Descent is only the expression for the continuity in the history of the race, which always moves by quantitative determinants and therefore is never capable of bringing forth an individual. For an animal species, even if it has preserved itself through a thousand and again another thousand generations, never brings forth an individual. If the second man had not descended from Adam, he would not have been the second man but an empty repetition, and from this would have been derived neither a race nor an individual. Every particular Adam would have been a statue by himself, and only to be defined by the indifferent specification, that is, by number, and that in a still more defective sense than when the Blue Boys[11] are designated by number. At the most, every particular man would have been himself, not himself and the race, and would have had no history, just as an angel has no history, is only himself and does not participate in any history.

It hardly need be said that this view is not chargeable with any sort of Pelagianism, which lets every individual, unconcerned about the race, play his own little history in his private theater; for the history of the race calmly pursues its course, and in this

---

* The contrast is expressed in §1: While the history of the race goes on, the individual constantly begins afresh.

no individual commences at the same place as another, whereas every individual begins afresh and that same instant is at the place where he ought to begin in history.

§3

The concept of innocence

IN THIS instance as usual, if one in our day would have a dogmatic definition, one must make a beginning by forgetting what Hegel invented in order to help dogmatics. One has a queer feeling when, in the dogmaticians who in other respects wish to be rather orthodox,[12] one sees Hegel's favorite remark[13] introduced, that the characteristic of the immediate is to be annulled (*aufgehoben*), as though immediacy and innocence were entirely identical. Hegel has quite consistently volatilized every dogmatic concept just far enough for it to support life in reduced circumstances as a *spirituel* expression for the logical. That the immediate needs to be annulled we do not need Hegel to tell us, neither does he deserve immortal merit for having said it, since, logically thought, it is not even correct; for the immediate may not be annulled, forasmuch as it never is [in the sense of *Dasein*]. The concept of immediacy properly belongs in logic, but the concept of innocence in ethics, and every concept must be dealt with as from that science to which it belongs, whether the concept belongs to the science in such a way that it is developed there, or is developed by being presupposed.

Now it is unethical to say that innocence must be annulled (*aufgehoben*), for even if it were annulled the instant this is uttered, ethics forbids us to forget that it can only be annulled by guilt. Therefore when one speaks of innocence as of immediacy, and is logically insolent and gruff enough to let this volatile thing have vanished, or aesthetically sentimental over what it was and that it has vanished, then one is only *geistreich* and forgets the point.

As Adam lost innocence by guilt, so does every man lose it. If it was not by guilt he lost it, neither was it innocence he lost; and if he was not innocent before he became guilty, he never became guilty.

As for Adam's innocence, there has been no lack of all sorts of fantastic conceptions, whether these attained symbolical sanction in times when the velvet on the church pulpit as well as on the beginnings of the race was not so frayed as it is now, or whether they roamed about romantically as the suspicious inventions of poetry. The more fantastically they managed to get Adam attired, the more inexplicable it became that he could sin, and the more frightful his sin became. He had however once and for all forfeited all the glory, and over that, according to time and circumstance, one became sentimental or witty, melancholy or frivolous, historically contrite or fantastically merry—but the point of it they did not grasp ethically.

As for the innocence of subsequent men (i.e. all with the exception of Adam and Eve), rather lowly notions have been entertained. Ethical rigorism ignored the limits of the ethical and was itself so upright as to believe that men would not seize the opportunity to give the slip to all that when escape was made so easy. Frivolity of course perceived nothing at all. But only by guilt is innocence lost; every man loses innocence in essentially the same way that Adam did, and it is not in the interest of ethics to represent all men as troubled and interested spectators of guilt, but not guilty, nor is it to the interest of dogmatics to represent all as interested and sympathetic spectators of redemption, but not redeemed.

If men have so often wasted the time of dogmatics and ethics, and their own time, by pondering about what would have happened in case Adam had not sinned, this merely shows that they have brought with them an incorrect mood and an incorrect concept. To the innocent man it never can occur to ask such a question, but the guilty man sins when he asks it; for with his aesthetic curiosity he would like to obscure the fact that he himself has brought guilt into the world, has himself lost innocence by guilt.

Innocence therefore is not some kind of immediacy which must be annulled (*aufgehoben*), the destination of which is to be annulled, something which properly speaking does not exist [in the sense of *Dasein*], but only comes into existence by the very fact that it is annulled, comes into existence as that which was before it was annulled and now is annulled. Immediacy is not annulled by mediacy, but when mediacy emerges it has that same instant annulled immediacy. The annulment of immediacy is therefore an immanent movement within immediacy, or it is an immanent movement in an opposite direction within mediacy, by which mediacy presupposes immediacy. Innocence is something which is annulled by transcendency, precisely because innocence is a *something* (whereas the correct expression for immediacy is that which Hegel[14] uses for pure being, saying that it is nothing), and for this reason also, when innocence is annulled by a transcendency, something quite different comes out of it, whereas mediacy is just immediacy. Innocence is a quality, it is a *state* which can very well endure, and therefore the logical haste to get it annulled is out of place, whereas immediacy in logic should try to hurry a little more, for it always arrives too late, even when it goes at full speed. Innocence is not a perfection one ought to wish to recover; for as soon as one wishes for it, it is lost, and it is a new guilt to waste time on wishes. Innocence is not an imperfection with which one cannot be content to stop but must go further; for innocence is always sufficient unto itself, and he who has lost it (lost it, that is to say, in the only way it can be lost, i.e. by guilt, and not in the way it perhaps pleases him to have lost it)—to that man it will not occur to boast of his perfection at the cost of innocence.

The account in Genesis gives also the right explanation of innocence. Innocence is ignorance. This is by no means the pure being of immediacy, but it is ignorance. The fact that ignorance regarded from without seems as though designed to become knowledge is entirely irrelevant to ignorance.

It is quite evident that this view is not tainted with Pelagianism. The race has its history, and within it sinfulness has its continuous quantitative modification, but invariably innocence is lost only by the qualitative leap of the individual. That this sinfulness which is the progression of the race may show itself as a greater or lesser disposition in the individual who by his act assumes it, is indeed true; but this is a more or less, a quantitative determination which does not constitute the concept of guilt.

§4

The concept of the Fall

IF THEN innocency is ignorance, it might seem that, inasmuch as the guiltiness of the race in its quantitative determination is present in the ignorance of the single individual and by his act manifests itself as his guiltiness, there must be a difference between Adam's innocence and that of every other man. The answer is already given, that a more does not constitute a quality. It might seem too that it would be easier to explain how a subsequent man lost innocence. This, however, is only apparently true. The highest degree of quantitative modification no more explains the qualitative leap than does the lowest. If I can explain guilt in the later man, I can equally well explain it in Adam. By habit, and still more by thoughtlessness and ethical stupidity, it has come to look as if the former were easier than the latter. One is so fain to avoid the sunstroke of consistency which falls directly upon the crown of one's head. One would put up with sinfulness, help to bear it, etc., etc. He need not give himself the pains. Sinfulness is not an epidemic which is transmitted like cowpox— "and every mouth shall be stopped." It is quite true that every man can say with profound seriousness that he was born in misery and his mother conceived him in sin; but really he can only sorrow rightly over it when he himself has brought guilt into the world and brought all this upon himself, for it is a contradiction to want to sorrow *aesthetically* over *sinfulness*. The only one who innocently sorrowed over sinfulness was Christ, but He did not sorrow over it as a destiny which He must put up with, but He sorrowed as one who freely chose to bear all the sin of the world and to suffer its punishment. This is not an aesthetic determinant, for Christ was more than an individual.

Innocence is ignorance—but how is it lost? It is not my intention to report here all the ingenious and absurd hypotheses by which the beginning of history has been encumbered by thinkers and speculators who only out of curiosity are interested in this great human affair we call "sin." I do not do so, partly because I would not waste other people's time by reciting that on the learning of which I have wasted my own time, and partly because the whole thing lies outside of history in the twilight where witches and speculators ride a race on broomsticks and sausage-pegs.

The science which has to do with the explanation is psychology, which, however, can only explain up to the explanation, and above all must guard against seeming to explain what no science explains, and which only ethics explains further by presupposing it through what it owes to dogmatics. If one wants to take the psychological explanation and repeat it several times, and thereupon is of the opinion that it is not improbable that in this way sin came into the world, one has confounded everything. Psychology must stay within its bounds, and then its explanation must always have significance.

A psychological explanation of the Fall is well and clearly expressed in Usteri's exposition of the Pauline doctrine.[15] Theology has now become so speculative that it scorns this sort of thing. It is in fact much easier to explain that the immediate must be annulled; and what theology sometimes does is even more convenient, namely, at the decisive moment of the explanation to become invisible before the eyes of the speculative worshipers. Usteri's exposition is to the effect that the command itself prohibiting Adam to eat of the tree of knowledge engendered sin in him. It does not by any means ignore the ethical but admits that the prohibition merely predisposes, as it were, what breaks out in Adam's qualitative leap. I have no intention of stating this exposition of Usteri's more fully. Everyone has read it, or can read it, in the works of this author.*

The lack in this explanation is that it does not wish to be thoroughly psychological. This is not censure, for it did not wish to be that; it had set itself another task, that of expounding the doctrine of Paul and attaching itself to the Bible. But in this way the Bible has often had a harmful effect. In beginning a deliberation one has certain classical texts fixed in one's mind, and now one's explanation and knowledge remains no more than an arrangement of these texts, as if the whole subject were so foreign to one. The more natural the better, even though one is willing with all deference to confront one's explanation with the judgment of the Scriptures, and, if it does not stand the test, tries to explain again. In this way one does not get into the preposterous position of having

* Everyone who would think seriously upon the present theme must of course know what Fr. Baader[16] has set forth with his usual pith and authority in several books dealing with the significance of temptation for the consolidation of freedom, as well as with the misunderstanding of conceiving temptation one-sidedly as only a temptation to evil, or that which has the purpose of making men fall, seeing that one must regard temptation rather as "the necessary other" of freedom. To recount this again is not necessary. Fr. Baader's works are in existence. Neither would it be appropriate here to follow his thought further, for it seems to me that Fr. Baader has overlooked intermediate determinants. The transition from innocence to guilt simply by means of the concept of temptation brings God into an almost experimental relation to man and overlooks the intermediate psychological observation, since after all the intermediate determinant is *concupiscentia*; and in fine his exposition is rather a dialectical reflection upon the concept of temptation than a psychological explanation of the more specific case.

to understand the explanation before one has understood what it is it is supposed to explain, nor into the disingenuous position of using Bible texts as the Persian king[17] used against the Egyptians their sacred animals to secure himself.

In making the prohibition the conditioning cause, one assumes that the prohibition awakens a *concupiscentia*. Here psychology has overstepped the bounds of its competence. A *concupiscentia* is a determinant of guilt and sin anterior to guilt and sin, to what therefore is not guilt and sin; that is to say, it is posited by them. The qualitative leap is enervated, the fall becomes something progressive. Nor does one see how the prohibition awakens *concupiscentia*, even though it is certain both from pagan and from Christian experience that man's desire is for the forbidden. But one cannot appeal thus without more ado to experience, since it rather might be asked in which period of life this is experienced. Nor is the intermediate determinant *concupiscentia* equivocal, and by this sign one sees at once that it is not the psychological explanation. The strongest and, I would say, the most positive expression the Protestant Church uses for the presence of original sin in man is precisely that he is born in *concupiscentia* (*Omnes homines secundum naturam propagati nascuntur cum peccato, h.e. sine metu dei, sine fiducia erga deum, et cum concupiscentia*).[18] And yet the Protestant doctrine assumes a difference between the innocence of the subsequent man (if there can properly be any question of such a thing) and the innocence of Adam.

The psychological explanation must not befuddle the point, but must remain in its elastic ambiguity, from which guilt breaks forth in the qualitative leap.

§5

The concept of dread

INNOCENCE is ignorance. In his innocence man is not determined as spirit but is soulishly determined in immediate unity with his natural condition. Spirit is dreaming in man. This view is in perfect accord with that of the Bible, and by refusing to ascribe to man in the state of innocence a knowledge of the difference between good and evil it condemns all the notions of merit Catholicism has imagined.

In this state there is peace and repose; but at the same time there is something different, which is not dissension and strife, for there is nothing to strive with. What is it then? Nothing. But what effect does nothing produce? It begets dread. This is the profound secret of innocence, that at the same time it is dread. Dreamingly the spirit projects its own reality, but this reality is nothing, but this nothing constantly sees innocence outside of it.

Dread is a qualification of the dreaming spirit, and as such it has its place in psychology. When awake, the difference between myself and my other[19] is posited; sleeping, it is suspended; dreaming, it is a nothing vaguely hinted at. The reality of the spirit constantly shows itself in a form which entices its possibility, but it is away as soon as one grasps after it, and it is a nothing which is able only to alarm. More it cannot do so long as it only shows itself. One almost never sees the concept dread dealt with in psychology, and I must therefore call attention to the fact that it is different from fear and similar concepts which refer to something definite, whereas dread is freedom's reality as possibility for possibility.[20] One does not therefore find dread in the beast, precisely for the reason that by nature the beast is not qualified by spirit.

When we consider the dialectical determinants in dread, it appears that they have precisely the characteristic ambiguity of psychology. Dread is a *sympathetic antipathy and an antipathetic sympathy*. One easily sees, I think, that this is much more truly a psychological subject than is the concupiscence of which we have spoken. Language confirms this completely. One speaks of a sweet dread, a sweet feeling of apprehension, one speaks of a strange dread, a shrinking dread, etc.

The dread which is posited in innocence is, in the first place, not guilt; in the second place, it is not a heavy burden, not a suffering which cannot be brought into harmony with the felicity of innocence. If we observe children, we find this dread more definitely indicated as a seeking after adventure, a thirst for the prodigious, the mysterious. The fact that there are children in whom this is not found proves nothing, for neither in the beast does it exist, and the less spirit, the less dread. This dread belongs to the child so essentially that it cannot do without it; even though it alarms him, it captivates him nevertheless by its sweet feeling of apprehension. In all nations in which the childish character is preserved as the dreaming of the spirit this dread is found, and the deeper it is, the more profound is the nation. It is only a prosaic stupidity which thinks that this is a disorganization. Dread has here the same significance melancholy has at a far later point where freedom, after having passed through imperfect forms of its history, has to come to itself in a deeper sense.*

Just as the relation of dread to its object, to something which is nothing (language in this instance also is pregnant: it speaks of being in dread of nothing), is altogether ambiguous, so will the transition here from innocence to guilt be correspondingly so dialectical that the explanation is and must be psychological. The qualitative leap is outside of ambiguity, but he who through dread becomes guilty is innocent, for it was not he himself but dread, an alien power, which laid hold of him, a power he did not love but dreaded—and yet he is guilty, for he sank in the dread which he loved even while he feared it. There is nothing in the world more ambiguous, and therefore this is the only psychological explanation, although (to repeat what I have said) it never occurs to it to want to be the explanation which explains the qualitative leap. Every theory about the prohibition tempting Adam or the seducer deceiving him has only for a superficial observation sufficient ambiguity, while it perverts ethics, introduces a quantitative determination, and would by the help of psychology pay man a compliment from which everyone who is ethically developed would beg to be excused, regarding it as a new and deeper seduction.

Everything turns upon dread coming into view. Man is a synthesis of the soulish and the bodily. But a synthesis is unthinkable if the two are not united in a third factor. This third factor is the spirit. In the state of innocence man is not merely an animal, for if at any time of his life he was merely an animal, he never would become a man. So then the spirit is present, but in a state of immediacy, a dreaming state. Forasmuch as it is present, it is in one way a hostile power, for it constantly disturbs the relation between soul and body, a relation which endures, and yet does not endure, inasmuch as it has endurance only by means of the spirit. On the other hand, it is a friendly power which has precisely the function of constituting the relationship. What then is man's relation to

* With regard to this one may consult *Either/Or* (Copenhagen 1843), noting especially that Part I represents melancholy, in its anguished sympathy and egotism, which in Part II is explained.

this ambiguous power? How is spirit related to itself and to its situation? It is related as dread. The spirit cannot do away with itself; nor can it grasp itself so long as it has itself outside of itself. Neither can man sink down into the vegetative life, for he is determined as spirit. He cannot flee from dread, for he loves it; really he does not love it, for he flees from it. Innocence has now reached its apex. It is ignorance, but not an animal brutality, but an ignorance which is qualified by spirit, but which precisely is dread, because its ignorance is about nothing. Here there is no knowledge of good and evil, etc., but the whole reality of knowledge is projected in dread as the immense nothing of ignorance.

Innocence still *is*, but one word suffices, and with that ignorance is concentrated. Innocence of course cannot understand this word; but dread has as it were obtained its first prey; instead of nothing, innocence gets an enigmatic word. So when it is related in Genesis that God said to Adam, "Only of the tree of the knowledge of good and evil thou shalt not eat," it is a matter of course that Adam did not really understand this word. For how could he have understood the difference between good and evil, seeing that this distinction was in fact consequent upon the enjoyment of the fruit?

When one assumes that the prohibition awakens the desire, one posits a knowledge instead of ignorance; for Adam would have had to have a knowledge of freedom, since his desire was to use it. The explanation therefore anticipates what was subsequent. The prohibition alarms Adam [induces a state of dread] because the prohibition awakens in him the possibility of freedom. That which passed innocence by as the nothing of dread has now entered into him, and here again it is a nothing, the alarming possibility of *being able*. What it is he is able to do, of that he has no conception; to suppose that he had some conception is to presuppose, as commonly is done, what came later, the distinction between good and evil. There is only the possibility of being able, as a higher form of ignorance, as a heightened expression of dread, because this in a more profound sense is and is not, because in a more profound sense he loves it and flees from it.

After the word of prohibition follows the word of judgment: "Thou shalt surely die." What it means to die, Adam of course cannot conceive; but if one assumes that these words were said to him, there is nothing to prevent his having a notion of the terrible. Indeed even the beast is able to understand the mimic expression and movement in the speaker's voice, without under-standing the word. In case one lets the prohibition awaken desire, one may also let the word about punishment awaken a deterring conception. However, this confuses things. The terrible becomes in this instance merely dread; for Adam has not understood what was said, and here again we have only the ambiguity of dread. The infinite possibility of being able (awakened by the prohibition) draws closer for the fact that this possibility indicates a possibility as its consequence.

Thus innocence is brought to its last extremity. It is in dread in relation to the prohibition and the punishment. It is not guilty, and yet it is in dread, as though it were lost.

Further than this psychology cannot go, but so far it can reach, and moreover it can verify this point again and again in its observation of human life.

Here in the conclusion I attached myself to the Biblical account. I let the voice of the prohibition and the punishment come from without. This naturally has tormented many thinkers. The difficulty, however, is one we need only smile at. Innocence is indeed well able to talk, inasmuch as in language it possesses the expression for everything in the spiritual order. In view of this one need only assume that Adam talked with himself. The imperfection in the account, that another speaks to Adam about what he does not understand, is thus eliminated. Adam was able to talk. From this it does not follow that in a deeper sense he was able to understand the word uttered. This applies above all to the distinction between good and evil, which is made in language, to be sure, but is only intelligible to freedom. Innocence can very well utter this distinction, but the distinction is not for it, and for it this has only the significance we have shown above.

§6

Dread as the presupposition of original sin and as explaining original sin retrogressively in the direction of its origin

LET us now examine the account of Genesis more closely, trying to put aside the fixed idea that it is a myth, and reminding ourselves that no age has been so intent upon producing myths as our own, which is producing myths at the same time that it wants to extirpate all myths.

So Adam was created, had bestowed names upon the animals (so here we have language, even though of a kind as imperfect as that of children when they are learning to recognize an animal on the ABC card), but had not found society for himself. Eve was created, formed from his rib. She stood in as intimate a relation to him as possible, and yet this was still an external relation. Adam and Eve are merely a numerical repetition. The existence in this sense of a thousand Adams signifies no more than one. This may be said in view of the descent of the race from one pair. Nature has no liking for a meaningless profusion. If therefore it is assumed that the race descends from several couples, there would have been a moment when nature had an unnecessary profusion. As soon as the fact of generation is posited no man is a superfluity, for every individual is himself and the race.

Then follows the prohibition and the judgment. But the serpent was more subtle than any beast of the field. He enticed woman. Even though one would call this a myth, one must remember that it does not disturb thought nor confuse the concept as a myth of the understanding does. The myth represents as outward that which occurred inwardly.

What first we have to remark upon here is that woman is first seduced, and that thereupon she seduces man. Subsequently in another chapter I seek to explain in what sense woman is the weaker sex, as is commonly said of her, and also to show that dread is more natural to her than to man.*

In the foregoing I have several times called attention to the fact that the view presented in this work does not deny the propagation of sinfulness through generation, or in other words that sinfulness has its history in the fact of generation; I have only said that sinfulness moves by quantitative determinants, whereas sin comes in constantly by the qualitative leap of the individual. Here one can already see one significance of the quantitative process of generation. Eve is the derived being. True, she is created like Adam, but she is created out of a precedent creature. True, she is innocent

---

* Nothing is determined by this about woman's imperfection in comparison with man. Even if dread is more natural to her than to man, dread is by no means a sign of imperfection. If there is to be any question of imperfection, it consists in something else, namely, in the fact that in dread she seeks support beyond herself in another, in man.

like Adam, but there is as it were a presentiment of a disposition, which indeed is not yet in existence, yet may seem like a hint of the sinfulness posited by reproduction. It is the fact of being derived which predisposes the individual, without for all that making him guilty.

What was said in §5 about the word of prohibition and judgment must be recalled here. The imperfection in the account, the doubt how it could have occurred to anyone to say to Adam what he cannot understand, is eliminated when one reflects that the speaker is language, and that hence it is Adam himself who speaks.*

Now remains the serpent. I am no lover of *esprit*, and *volente Deo* I shall withstand the temptation of that serpent who, as at the beginning of time he tempted Eve, has in the course of time tempted writers to be *spirituel*. I prefer to admit bluntly that I can associate no definite thought with the serpent. The difficulty about the serpent moreover is quite a different one, namely, that it lets the temptation come from without. This conflicts directly with the teaching of the Bible, with the well-known classical passage in St. James affirming that God tempts no man and also is tempted by no one, but that every man is tempted by himself. For when one thinks that one has rescued God by letting man be tempted by the serpent, and that thus one is in accord with St. James's saying, that God tempts no man, one then collides with the second saying, that God is not tempted by anyone, for the serpent's temptation of man was at the same time an indirect temptation directed against God, by mixing himself up in the relation between God and man; and one collides with the third saying, that every man is tempted by himself. In short, the hill of the serpent.

Then follows the Fall. This is what psychology is unable to explain, for it is the qualitative leap. But let us for a moment consider the consequence as it is reported in the narrative, in order to fix attention once again upon dread as the presupposition of original sin.

The consequence was a double one: that sin came into the world,

* If one would say further that there then remains the question how the first man learned to speak, then I will reply that this is quite true, but I would say also that the question lies outside the compass of this investigation. This, however, must not be understood, as though in the manner of modern philosophy I would by making this reply pretend that I *could* answer this question in another place. But so much is sure, that it does not do to represent that man himself invented language.

and that sexuality was posited—the one being inseparable from the other. This is of the utmost importance in order to show what was man's original state. For if in fact he was not a synthesis which reposes in a third factor, one thing could not have two consequences. If he were not a synthesis of soul and body which is sustained by spirit, the sexual could never come into the world with sinfulness.

We will leave speculators[21] out of account and simply assume the presence of sexual differentiation before the Fall, with the observation however that it did not strictly exist, because it does not exist in ignorance. In this respect we have support in the Scripture.

In his innocence man was, in so far as he was spirit, a dreaming spirit. The synthesis therefore is not actual; for the combining factor is precisely the spirit, and this is not yet posited as spirit. In the animal sexual diversity can be developed instinctively; but in this way man cannot have it, precisely because he is a synthesis. The instant the spirit posits itself it posits the synthesis, but to posit the synthesis it must first permeate it differentially, and the extremest expression of the sensuous is precisely the sexual. This extreme man can attain only at the instant when the spirit becomes actual. Before that time he is not an animal, but neither is he properly a man. The instant he becomes a man he becomes such only by being at the same time an animal.

Sinfulness then is not sensuousness, not by any means; but without sin there is no sexuality, and without sexuality no history. A perfect spirit has neither the one nor the other, hence also the sexual difference is annulled in the resurrection, and hence too no angel has history. Even though the archangel Michael had recorded all the missions on which he was sent and which he performed, this nevertheless is not his history. The synthesis is first posited in the sexual as a contradiction, but at the same time, like every contradiction, as a task, the history of which begins that very instant. This is the actuality which is preceded by the possibility of freedom. But the possibility of freedom does not consist in being able to choose the good or the evil. Such thoughtlessness has as little support in the Scripture as in philosophy. Possibility means *I can*. In a logical system it is convenient enough to say that possibility passes over into actuality. In reality it is not so easy, and an intermediate determinant is necessary. This intermediate determinant is dread, which no more explains the qualitative leap than it justifies it ethically. Dread is not a determinant of necessity, but neither is it of freedom; it is a trammeled freedom, where freedom is not free in itself but trammeled, not by necessity but in itself. If sin has come into the world by necessity (which is a self-contradiction), then there is no dread. If sin has come into the world by an act of abstract *liberum arbitrium* (which no more existed at the beginning than it does at a later period of the world, for it is a non-sense to thought[22]), neither in this case is there dread. To want to explain logically the entrance of sin into the world is a stupidity which could only occur to people who are comically anxious to get an explanation.

If I were allowed to make a wish, I would wish that no reader might be profound enough to ask the question, "If then Adam had not sinned?" The moment reality is posited, possibility steps to one side as a nothing which serves as a temptation to all men devoid of thought. What a pity science cannot resolve to keep people under discipline and to keep itself in check! When someone asks a stupid question, we should take heed not to answer him, for if we do we are as stupid as the questioner. The foolishness of that question consists not so much in the question itself as in the fact that it is addressed to science. When one stays at home with it, like the shrewd Else[23] with her projects, and calls together like-minded friends, it is a sign that in some measure one has understood one's stupidity. Science cannot explain such things. Every science has its province either in immanent logic, or in an immanence within a transcendence which it cannot explain. Now sin is precisely that transcendence, that *discrimen rerum*, by which sin enters into the individual as an individual. In no other way does sin enter the world, and never has it entered otherwise. When the individual then is foolish enough to inquire about sin as about something irrelevant to him, he speaks as a fool; for either he does not know in the least what the question is about and cannot possibly learn to know it, or else he knows it and understands it, and knows too that no science can explain it. Nevertheless science has sometimes been accommodating enough to respond to sentimental wishes with deeply pondered hypotheses, which, as science itself admits, do not adequately explain. This is quite true, but the confusion is due to the fact that science did not energetically repel foolish questions, that on the contrary it confirmed superstitious people in the notion that some day there would come a scientific speculator who would be <u>man enough</u> to hit upon the right answer. They speak about sin coming into the world 6000 years ago, just as they speak about Nebuchadnezzar becoming an ox 4000 years ago.[24] When they conceive the case thus, what wonder the explanation is no better? That which in one sense is the simplest thing in the world, they have made the most difficult. That which the simplest man understands in his way, and quite rightly, for he understands that it is not exactly 6000 years ago sin came into the world, this thing science by the aid of the speculator's art has propounded as a prize question which has never yet been satisfactorily answered. <u>How sin came into the world every man understands by himself alone; if he would learn it from</u> another, he <u>eo ipso</u> misunderstands it. The only science which can do a little is psychology, which nevertheless concedes that it does not, that it can and will not, explain more. If any science could explain it, everything would be brought to confusion. That the man of science ought to forget himself is perfectly true, but for this reason it is so fortunate that sin is not a scientific problem, and therefore the man of science is no more obliged than is any speculator to forget how sin came into the world. If he would do that, if he would magnanimously forget himself, he with his zeal to explain humanity as a whole becomes just as ridiculous as the privy counselor who sacrificed himself to such a degree in leaving his visiting cards on Tom, Dick and Harry, that in doing so he finally forgot his own name. Or else his philosophical enthusiasm makes him so forgetful of himself that he is in need of an honest and sober wedded wife of whom he can ask as the bookseller Soldin[25] asked Rebecca when he also in enthusiastic self-forgetfulness had lost himself in the objectivity of twaddle, "Rebecca, is it I that am speaking?"

That the admired men of science in this respected generation to which I have the honor to belong will find this chapter exceedingly unscientific is a matter of course. In their concern for and search after the System they are naturally concerned, as the whole congregation knows, to find a place in it for sin too. Only let the congregation join in the search, or at least include these profound seekers in their pious intercessions; they will find the place as surely as he who hunts for the burning tow finds it when he takes no heed that it is burning his own hand.

CHAPTER II

Dread as Original Sin Progressively

WITH sinfulness was posited sexuality. That same instant the history of the race begins. Since sinfulness moves by quantitative increments, so does dread also. The consequence of original sin or of its presence in the individual is dread, which only quantitatively is different from that of Adam. In the state of innocence, and of that we may speak in the case of the later man, original sin must have the dialectical ambiguity out of which guilt breaks forth in the qualitative leap. On the other hand, dread in the later individual can possibly be more reflective than in Adam, because the quantitative increment accumulated by the race now makes itself felt in him. Dread, however, is no more than it was before an imperfection in man; on the contrary, one may say that the more primitiveness a man has, the deeper is the dread, because the presupposition of sinfulness which his individual life supposes, since he enters indeed into the history of the race, must be appropriated. Sinfulness has thus acquired a great power, and original sin is growing. That there are people who do not notice any dread must be understood in the sense that Adam would have sensed none if he had been merely an animal.

The later individual is like Adam a synthesis which must be sustained by spirit; but this synthesis is derived, and owing to that the history of the race is constantly posited by it. This accounts for the more or less dread in the later individual. His dread, however, is not a dread of sin, for the distinction between good and evil first comes about with the actuality of freedom. If this distinction is present, it is only a vague presentiment, which in the course of the history of the race may again mean a more or a less.

The fact that dread in the later individual is more reflective as a consequence of his participation in the history of the race, comparable in a way to habit which is, as it were, man's second nature, yet not a new quality but only a quantitative progress—this fact, I say, is accounted for by the consideration that dread now enters the world with another significance. Sin entered by dread, but sin in turn brought dread with it. In point of fact the reality of sin is a reality which has no continuous endurance. On the one hand, the continuity of sin is the possibility which causes dread; on the other hand, the possibility of a salvation is a nothing which again the individual both loves and fears; for this is always the relation of possibility to individuality. It is only at the instant when salvation is actually posited that this dread is overcome. The longing of man and of the whole creation[1] is not, as men have sentimentally thought, a sweet longing, for merely in order that this might be so, sin must be disarmed. The man who will realize truly what the state of sin is, and how the expectation of salvation must be felt, will certainly concede this and will be a little bit embarrassed at aesthetic unembarrassment. Sin in man still has power so long as it is only a question of expectation, and naturally it construes this expectation hostilely. (This will be dealt with later.[2]) When salvation is posited, dread is put behind, just as possibility is. With this it is not annihilated but now plays another role, if it is rightly used (cf. Chapter V).

The dread which sin brings with it exists in the strictest sense only when the individual himself posits sin, but nevertheless it is obscurely present as a more or less in the quantitative history of the race. Hence even here one will encounter the phenomenon that a man seems to become guilty merely for dread of himself, of which there could be no question in the case of Adam. That every individual becomes guilty only by his own act is nevertheless perfectly certain; but the quantitative process involved in generation has here reached its maximum where it would have power to confuse every view if one does not hold fast to the difference already pointed out between the quantitative increment and the qualitative leap. This phenomenon will be dealt with later. Generally it is ignored. That is in fact the easiest way. Or it is construed sentimentally and emotionally with a cowardly sympathy which thanks God for not being like such a man, without comprehending that such an act of thanksgiving is treason against God and against oneself, and without reflecting that life has always in store analogous phenomena which perhaps one will not escape. Sympathy one must have; but this sympathy is genuine only when one knows oneself deeply and knows that what has happened to one man may happen to all. Only thus can one be of some utility to oneself and to others. The physician in an insane asylum who is foolish enough to believe that he is wise for all eternity and that his bit of reason is insured against all injury in life, is indeed in

a certain sense wiser than the crazy patients, but at the same time
he is more foolish, and he surely will not heal many.

So then dread signifies two things: the dread in which the individual posits sin by the qualitative leap; and the dread which
entered in along with sin, and which for this reason comes also
into the world quantitatively every time an individual posits sin.

It is not my purpose to write a learned work or to waste time
looking up literary proof texts. Oftentimes the examples adduced
in books on psychology lack the proper psychological-poetic authority. They stand there as isolated facts notarially attested, but
precisely for this reason one does not know whether to laugh or
weep at the attempt of such a lonely stickler to form some sort of a
general rule. A man who with any degree of seriousness has concerned himself with psychology and psychological observations has
acquired a general human pliability which makes him capable of
being able to construct his example at once, one which, even though
it has not authorization of the factual sort, has nevertheless a different kind of authority. As the psychological observer ought to
be more agile than the tightrope dancer in order to be able to in-
sinuate himself under the skin of other people and to imitate their
attitudes, as his silence in confidential moments ought to be seductive and voluptuous in order that the hidden thing may find pleasure in slipping out and chatting quietly with itself in this fictitious
inattention and quiet, so he ought also to have a poetical primitiveness in his soul to be able to create at once the totality of the rule
out of that which in the individual is always present only partially
and irregularly. Then when he has perfected himself he will not
need to fetch his examples from literary repertoires and warmed-
over, half-dead reminiscences but draws his observations directly
and freshly from the water, still flopping and displaying the play
of their colors. Neither will he need to run himself to death in
order to make note of something. On the contrary, he will sit
calmly in his chamber, like a detective who knows nevertheless
everything that is going on. What he needs he is able to fashion
at once; what he needs he has straightway at hand by virtue of
his general practice, just as in a well-ordered house one does not
need to go down to the street to fetch water but has it on his floor
by high pressure. If he were to become doubtful, he is then so
well oriented in human life and his glance is so inquisitorially sharp

that he knows where he should seek and easily discover some individual or another who would be serviceable for his experiment. His observation will be as trustworthy as that of any other man, even though he does not support it with erudite quotations—for example, that in Saxony there was a peasant girl whom a physician had under observation, that in Rome there was an emperor of whom a historian relates, etc.—as though it were true that such things emerge only once every thousand years. What interest has it then for psychology? No, it is everywhere, occurs every day, if only an observer is there. His observation will have the stamp of freedom and the interest of reality, if he is prudent enough to verify it. To this end he imitates in his own person every mood, every psychic state, which he discovers in another. Thereupon he sees if he cannot delude the other by his imitation, whether he can draw him into the further development which is his own creation by virtue of the idea. Thus if one would observe a passion, one has to choose one's individual. Then the thing is to be quiet silent, unobtrusive, so that one may lure the secret from him. Thereupon one practices what one has learned until one is able to deceive him. Thereupon one poetizes the passion and appears before him in passion's preternatural size. If this is done correctly, the individual will feel an indescribable relief and satisfaction, as does a demented man when one has found and poetically comprehended his fixed idea and then develops it further. If this does not succeed, the failure may be due to a fault in the operation, but it may also be due to the fact that the individual was a poor example.

§1

Objective dread

WHEN we use the expression "objective dread" one might be led to think more especially of the dread felt by innocence, which is the reflex of freedom within itself at the thought of its possibility. To this notion it is not a sufficient objection that it overlooks the consideration that we have reached a different point in the investigation. It might be more serviceable to note that objective dread is here contrasted with subjective dread, and that this is a distinction which could not have been made in Adam's state of innocence. Taken in the strictest sense, subjective dread is the dread posited in the individual as the consequence of his sin. About that we shall speak in a subsequent chapter. But when the term is taken in this sense, the contrast with an objective dread vanishes, since dread manifests itself precisely as that which it is, namely, the subjective. The distinction between the subjective and the objective dread has its place therefore in the contemplation of the world and of the state of innocence of the later individual. The division occurs here in such a way that subjective dread now designates the dread which exists in the innocence of the individual, a dread which corresponds to that of Adam and yet is quantitatively different from Adam's by reason of the quantitative increment due to generation. By objective dread, on the other hand, we understand the reflection in the whole world of that sinfulness which is propagated by generation.

In §2 of the previous chapter it was observed that the proposition, "by Adam's sin came sinfulness *into the world*," contained an external reflection; here is the place to take up that expression again and examine what truth there may be in it. The instant Adam has posited sin our reflection leaves him and reflects upon the beginning of the sin of every subsequent individual; for now generation is posited. If by Adam's sin the sinfulness of the race is posited in the same sense that man's erect posture, etc., is due to him, then the concept of the individual is annulled. This has been shown in the foregoing discussion, where also a protest was made against the inquisitive experimentation which treats sin as a curiosity, and the dilemma was put that we must either imagine a questioner who did not even know what he was questioning about, or else a questioner who knows it and whose pretended ignorance constitutes a new sin.

If now we hold fast to this, the expression I have referred to acquires a limited degree of truth. The first posits the quality. Adam, then, posits sin in himself but also for the race. But the concept of race is altogether too abstract to be capable of positing so concrete a category as sin, which precisely is posited by the fact that the individual himself posits it as the individual. Sinfulness in the race therefore is only a quantitative approximation, but it has its beginning in Adam. In this consists the great importance Adam has above every other individual in the race; and in this consists the truth of that expression. Even an orthodoxy which is willing to understand itself must concede this, for it teaches in fact that by Adam's sin nature as well as the human race falls under sin. But with relation to nature it surely will not do to say that sin had entered into it with the quality of sin.

By the fact then that sin came into the world, it acquired significance for the whole creation. This effect of sin in the non-human sphere of being I have called objective dread.

I can indicate what I mean by recalling the Scriptural expression in Romans 8:19; ἀποκαραδοκία τῆς κτίσεως (the anxious longing of creation). For if there can properly be any question of anxious longing, it follows as a matter of course that the creation is in a state of imperfection. When one uses such expressions as longing, anxious longing, expectation, etc., one commonly overlooks the fact that they imply a precedent state, and hence that this is present and makes itself felt at the same time that longing develops. The state in which the expectant man is, he has not fallen into by accident, etc., so that he finds himself entirely strange in it, but he himself is at the same time producing it. The expression for such a longing is dread, for in dread the state out of which a man longs to be delivered announces itself, and it announces itself because longing alone is not enough to save the man.

The question in what sense the creation by reason of Adam's sin sank into perdition, or how it was that freedom, being posited by the fact that the misuse of it posited it, cast over the whole creation a reflection of possibility and a shudder of complicity; in what sense this must occur because man is a synthesis whose extremest contrasts were posited and whose one contrast became precisely by man's sin a far more extreme contrast than it was before—all this finds no place in a psychological deliberation, but rather in dogmatics, in the doctrine of the Atonement, in the explanation of this the science of psychology explains the presupposition of sinfulness.*

Surely this dread in the creation can rightly be called an objective dread. It was not produced by the creation but was produced by the fact that it is seen in an entirely different light which was shed upon it when by Adam's first sin sensuality was degraded to signify sinfulness and is constantly so degraded in so far as sin

---

* It is in this way dogmatics must be planned. Every science must above all comprehend energetically its own proper beginning, and not live in a relation of prolix intercourse with the other sciences. If dogmatics begins by wanting to explain sinfulness, or by wanting to prove its reality, no dogmatic will ever come out of it, and its whole existence will become problematic and vague.

continues to come into the world. One easily sees that this interpretation has its eyes open also in this sense, that it parries the rationalistic view that the sensual itself is sinful. After sin has come into the world, and every time sin comes into the world, sensuality becomes sinful; but what becomes was not beforehand what it became. Fr. Baader has often protested against this proposition that man's pitiful condition, that the sensual as such, is sinfulness. If, however, one does not take care, one falls into Pelagianism on quite a different side. In point of fact, Fr. Baader[3] in his definition has not taken into account the history of the race. In the quantitative becoming of the race (therefore unessentially) sensuality is sinfulness; but it is not so in relation to the individual before he himself by positing sin again makes sensuality sinful.

Individual exponents[4] of the school of Schelling* have given special attention to the alteration† which has taken place in the creation by reason of sin. They have also spoken of the dread that

* Schelling himself often talks about dread, wrath, anguish, suffering, etc. However, one ought always to maintain an attitude of distrust towards such words, in order not to confound the consequence of sin in the creation with what Schelling also designates as states of mind and feelings in God. As a matter of fact, by these expressions he designates, if I dare say so, the creative birth-pangs of the Deity. He indicates by figurative expressions what he himself has called "the negative" and which in Hegel[5] became "the negative more closely defined as the dialectical" ($\tau o\ \text{ἕτερον}$). The ambiguity appears also in Schelling, for he speaks of a melancholy[6] brooding over nature, and also of a sadness in the Deity. However, Schlegel's ruling thought for the most part is that dread, etc., designates principally the sufferings of the Deity trying to create. In Berlin he expressed the same thought still more definitely by comparing God with Goethe and Johannes von Müller, who only found themselves by producing; as he did also by calling attention to the fact that blessedness which is unable to impart itself is unblessedness. I mention this here because this saying of his has already been printed in a little pamphlet by Marheineke.[7] Marheineke would treat it ironically. That one should not do, for a vigorous and full-blooded anthropomorphism is worth a good deal. In fact, the fault is a different one, and by this example one may see how strange everything becomes when metaphysics and dogmatics are corrupted by treating dogmatics metaphysically and metaphysics dogmatically.

† [In Danish] the word "alteration"[8] expresses the ambiguity very well. In fact one uses the word in the sense of changing, distorting, bringing out of the original state (the thing becomes a different one) ; but one also speaks of becoming *altereret* in the sense of becoming frightened, precisely because at bottom this is the first unavoidable consequence of change. So far as I know the word is not used at all in Latin, but curiously enough the word *adulterare* is used. The Frenchman says, *"altérer les monnaies"* and *"être altéré."* With us [in Denmark] the word is generally employed in everyday speech only in the sense of being afraid; and so one may hear the plain man say, "I was quite *altereret*." At least I have heard a street-vendor say it.

is supposed to be in inanimate nature. However the effect is weakened by the fact that at one moment we seem to have before us a dictum of natural philosophy which is handled cleverly by the aid of dogmatics, at another moment a dogmatic definition which rejoices in a glamorous reflection from the marvelous discoveries of natural science.

But here I abruptly terminate a disquisition which for an instant has transgressed the bounds of the present investigation. In the form in which dread existed in Adam it has never again appeared, for by him sinfulness came into the world. Consequently that dread of his has now acquired two analogous expressions: objective dread in nature, and subjective dread in the individual —of which two the latter contains a more and the former a less than that dread in Adam.

§2

Subjective dread

THE more reflective we venture to assume dread is, the easier it might seem to get it to pass over into guilt. But here it is important not to let ourselves be beguiled by gradual approximations, but to hold fast to the fact that it is not a "more" which gives rise to the leap, and that the "easier" does not in truth make the explanation easier. If we do not hold fast to this, we run the risk of stumbling suddenly upon a phenomenon where everything goes so easily that the transition becomes a simple transition, or else the risk of never daring to bring our thought to a conclusion, because the purely empirical observation can never be finished. Therefore, even though the dread become more and more reflective, the guilt which breaks forth in dread by the qualitative leap retains nevertheless the same accountability as that of Adam, and dread retains the same ambiguity.

To wish to deny that every subsequent individual has or may be assumed to have had a state of innocence analogous to that of Adam, would not only offend every man but would abrogate all rational thought, because then there would be an individual who was not an individual but was related as a sample to the species, in spite of the fact that at the same time he would be viewed under the category of the individual, that is, as a guilty man.

One may liken dread to dizziness. He whose eye chances to look down into the yawning abyss becomes dizzy. But the reason for it is just as much his eye as it is the precipice. For suppose he had not looked down.

Thus dread is the dizziness of freedom which occurs when the spirit would posit the synthesis, and freedom then gazes down into its own possibility, grasping at finiteness to sustain itself. In this dizziness freedom succumbs. Further than this psychology cannot go and will not. That very instant everything is changed, and when freedom rises again it sees that it is guilty. Between these two instants lies the leap, which no science has explained or can explain. He who becomes guilty in dread becomes as ambiguously guilty as it is possible to be. Dread is a womanish debility in which freedom swoons. Psychologically speaking, the fall into sin always occurs in impotence. But dread is at the same time the most egoistic thing, and no concrete expression of freedom is so egoistic as is the possibility of every concretion. This again is the overwhelming experience which determines the individual's ambiguous relation, both sympathetic and antipathetic. In dread there is the egoistic infinity of possibility, which does not tempt like a definite choice, but alarms (*ængster*) and fascinates with its sweet anxiety (*Beængstelse*).

In the later individual dread is more reflective. This may be expressed by saying that the nothing which is the object of dread becomes, as it were, more and more a something. We do not say that it really becomes something or really signifies something, we do not say that now instead of nothing there should be substituted sin or something else, for here what was true of Adam's innocence is true also of the later individual. All this applies only to freedom, and only when the individual himself by the qualitative leap posits sin. Here then the nothing of dread is a complex of presentiments which reflect themselves in themselves, coming nearer and nearer to the individual, notwithstanding that in dread they signify again essentially nothing, not, however, be it noted, a nothing with which the individual has nothing to do, but a nothing in lively communication with the ignorance of innocence. This reflectiveness is a predisposition which, before the individual becomes guilty, signifies essentially nothing, whereas when by the qualitative leap he becomes guilty it is the presupposition in which the individual goes beyond himself because sin presupposes itself, not of course before

it is posited (that would be a predestination), but presupposes itself when it is posited.

We shall now consider a little more particularly that *something*
which the nothing of dread may signify in the later individual.
In the psychological deliberation it truly counts for something. But
the psychological deliberation does not forget that if the individual
were to become guilty simply by this something, then all reflection
would be annulled.

This something, which signifies original sin *stricte sic dicta*, is:

A. THE CONSEQUENCE OF THE FACT OF GENERATION

It is a matter of course that nothing is to be said here about subjects which might concern a physician, like the fact that a man is
born with a deformity, etc., neither should there be any question
of reaching a result by statistical surveys. Here as in all such cases
the point is to have a right sentiment. Thus, for example, when it
is affirmed that hail and a failure of the crops is due to the devil,
this may be very well meant, but essentially it is a witty remark
which weakens our conception of evil and introduces an almost
jesting note, just as it is an aesthetic pleasantry to talk of the
"dumb devil." Thus too when in the concept of faith the historical
factor is stressed so one-sidedly that we forget the pristine originality of faith in the individual, it becomes a petty finiteness instead of a free infinitude. The consequence of this is that one may
become accustomed to talk about faith as did Jeronymus in Heiberg's play,[9] who says of Erasmus that he had opinions which lead
astray from faith, because he affirmed that the earth is round, not
flat as one generation after another in his village had believed. In
that way one can stray from faith by wearing loose trousers when
all the people in that village wear tight pants. When one furnishes
statistical surveys of the incidence of sinfulness, with maps in
color and relief which help the eye at once to make the survey,
one attempts by that to deal with sin as a curious phenomenon of
nature, which is not to be removed but only calculated, like the at-
mospheric pressure and the rainfall; and the mean or mathematical
average which results is here an absurdity which has no parallel
in those purely empirical sciences. It surely would be a very ludicrous abracadabra if one were to say that the mathematical average is 3 3/8 inches of sinfulness for each man, that in Languedoc

it comes to only 2 1/4, but in Brittany to 3 7/8.—These examples are no more superfluous that those given in the Introduction, since they are drawn from the sphere within the limits of which the following argument is to move.

By sin sensuousness became sinfulness. This proposition has a double significance: by sin sensuousness became sinfulness; and by Adam sin came into the world. These definitions must constantly balance one another, for otherwise something untrue is said. The fact that once upon a time sensuousness became sinfulness is the history of generation; but that sensuousness continues to become this is due to the qualitative leap of the individual.

It was observed in Chapter I, §6, that the creation of Eve already prefigured symbolically the consequence of generation. In a way she represented the derived individual. The derived is never as perfect as the original.* In this case, however, the difference is only quantitative. The later individual is essentially as original as the first. The difference common to all later individuals is derivation; but for the particular individual derivation may again signify more or less.

This derivation of woman explains also in what sense she is weaker than man, a fact which has been assumed in all times, whether it is a pasha who speaks or a romantic knight. The difference, however, does not mean that man and woman are not essentially alike in spite of the difference. The expression for the difference is that dread is more reflected in Eve than in Adam. This is due to the fact that woman is more sensuous than man. Here of course it is not a question of an empirical condition or of an average but of a difference in the synthesis. If in one part of the synthesis there is a "more," the consequence will be that when the spirit posits itself the cleft in the division will be more profound, and dread will find in the possibility of freedom more ample scope. In the account in Genesis it is Eve who seduces Adam. From this it does not by any means follow that her guilt is greater than Adam's, and still less that dread is an imperfection, since on the contrary the greatness of it is prophetically a measure of the perfection.

---

* Of course this holds true only of the human race, because the individual is characterized as spirit. On the other hand, in animal species every later example is just as good as the first, or, to put it better, to be the first has no significance whatsoever.

Here already the investigation sees that sensuousness corresponds proportionally with dread. As soon as generation is posited what was said about Eve is merely a hint of what is characteristic of the relation of every later individual to Adam, that when sensuousness is increased by the fact of generation dread also is increased. The consequence of generation signifies a "more," in such a way that no individual escapes from that "more" characteristic of all individuals in comparison with Adam, but never does it amount to such a "more" that he becomes essentially different from Adam.

But before we go on to speak of this I would illustrate a little more fully the proposition that woman is more sensuous than man and has more dread.

The fact that woman is more sensuous than man is shown at once by her bodily organism. To follow this out more in detail is not my affair but is a theme for physiology. I shall prove my thesis, however, in a different way, by introducing her aesthetically in her ideal aspect, which is beauty, noting that the fact that this *is* her ideal aspect is precisely the proof that she is more sensuous than man. Next I shall introduce her ethically in her ideal aspect, noting that the fact that this is her ideal aspect is precisely the proof that she is more sensuous than man.

Where beauty claims the right to rule it brings about a synthesis from which spirit is excluded. This is the secret of the whole Hellenic culture. Owing to this there is a sense of security, a quiet solemnity, which characterizes all Greek beauty; but precisely for this cause there was also a sense of dread, which the Greek likely did not notice, although his plastic beauty trembles with it. There is a carefreeness in the Greek beauty because the spirit is excluded, but therefore there is also a profound sorrow unexplained. Therefore sensuousness is not sinfulness but an unexplained riddle which causes dread; therefore this naïveté is accompanied by an inexplicable nothing which is that of dread.

It is true that the Greek beauty conceives man and woman essentially in the same way, without consideration of spirit; but nevertheless it makes a distinction within this likeness. The spiritual finds expression in the countenance. But in manly beauty the face and its expression are more essential than in feminine beauty, even though the eternal youth of the plastic art constantly prevents the deeper spiritual meaning from showing itself. To follow this out further is not my affair, but I will indicate this difference by a single suggestion. Essentially Venus remains equally beautiful whether she is represented sleeping or waking—indeed, she is perhaps most beautiful sleeping, and yet the sleeping state is precisely the expression for the absence of spirit. Hence it comes that the more spiritual and developed an individuality is, the less beautiful is such a person in sleep, whereas the child is most beautiful in sleep. Venus emerges from the sea and is represented in an attitude of repose, or in an attitude which reduces the expression of the face to the unessential. On the other hand, if Apollo is to be represented, it would not do to let him sleep, any more than in a Jupiter this would be appropriate. This would detract from the beauty of Apollo, and it would make Jupiter ridiculous. An exception could be made for Bacchus, but in Greek art he represents the point of indifference between manly and womanly beauty, and hence the lines of his figure are feminine. In the case of a Ganymede, on the other hand, the expression of his face is more essential.

When the conception of beauty became different, Romanticism again made the distinction within the essential likeness. Whereas the history of spirit (and it is precisely the secret of spirit that it always has history) dares to stamp itself upon the countenance of man, so that all is forgotten if only its writing is clear and noble, woman will make her effect in another way, as a totality, even though the face has acquired a greater importance than it had in classical art. The impression now must be of a totality which has no history. Therefore silence is not only woman's highest wisdom, but also her highest beauty.

Ethically regarded, woman culminates in procreation. Therefore the Scripture says that her desire shall be to her husband. It is true also that the husband's desire is to her, but his life does not culminate in this desire, unless it is either a sorry sort of life or a lost life. But the fact that in this woman reaches her culmination shows that she is more sensuous.

Woman is more in dread than man. This is not implied in the fact that she has less physical strength, etc., for here there is no question about that sort of dread; but it is implied in the fact that she is more sensuous and yet essentially, like man, is qualified by spirit. What is so frequently said, that she is the weaker sex, leaves me completely indifferent, for notwithstanding this she might very well have less dread. Dread is constantly to be understood as oriented towards freedom. So when the story in Genesis, running directly counter to all analogies, represents woman as seducing man, this upon closer inspection appears nevertheless perfectly natural, for this seduction is precisely a feminine seduction, since in fact it was only through Eve that Adam was seduced by the serpent. In other instances of seduction, language, speaking of deluding, talking around, etc., ascribes superiority to man.

That which can be assumed as the result of all experience I shall show merely by an experimental observation. If I picture to myself a young and innocent girl and then let a man fasten upon her a look of desire, she experiences dread. Besides that she may be indignant, etc., but first she feels dread. If on the other hand I imagine that a woman fixes a desirous glance upon an innocent young man, his feeling will not be dread, but at the most a sense of abhorrence mingled with shame, precisely because he is more characterized by spirit.

By Adam's sin came sinfulness into the world, and sexuality, which came to signify for him sinfulness. The sexual was posited. There has been much twaddle in the world, both written and oral, about naïveté. However, only innocence is naïve, but it is also ignorant. As soon as the sexual is brought to consciousness, it is thoughtlessness, affectation, and sometimes worse, namely, a cover for lust, to want to talk about naïveté. But because man is no longer naïve it does not follow by any means that he sins. It is only that vapid coquettishness which allures men, precisely by drawing attention away from the true, the moral.

The whole question about the significance of the sexual, and its significance in the particular spheres, has undeniably been poorly answered until now, and above all it is very seldom answered with the right feeling. To utter witticisms about it is a lowly art, to admonish is not difficult, to preach about it in such a way as to leave out the difficulties is not hard to do, but to talk about it in a fashion truly humane is an art. To let the theater and the pulpit undertake the solution and do it in such a way that the one is embarrassed to say what the other says, with the consequence that the explanation of the one is in violent contradiction to that of the other, is really to give the thing up and leave to men the heavy burden, which we do not put out a finger to lift, of finding a meaning in both explanations while the respective masters constantly teach only the one or the other. This incongruity would surely have been noticed long ago if men in these times had not perfected themselves in thoughtlessness directed to wasting this life so full of fair promise, or to taking part noisily whenever there is a question of one grand, prodigious idea or another, for the execution of which they unite with unshakable faith in the power of union, even though this faith is just as marvelous as that of the alehouse keeper who sold his ale for a penny less than he paid for it and yet reckoned upon a profit, "for it is the *many* that will do it." Such being the case, it will not surprise me if in these times no one pays any attention to such a deliberation. But this I know, that if Socrates were now living, he would think about such things, doing it better or, if I may say so, more divinely than I am able to do it, and I am convinced that he would have said to me, "My dear, you do well to think about such things, which are worthy of being reflected upon. Ah! one can sit talking night after night and never be through with fathoming the wonders of human nature. And to me this assurance is worth more than all the bravos of my contemporaries; for this assurance makes my soul firm, applause would make it doubtful."

The sexual itself is not the sinful. Real ignorance of the sexual, when nonetheless it is present, is reserved for the beast, which therefore is enthralled in the blindness of instinct and acts blindly. An ignorance, but now one which is ignorant of that which is not present, is that of the child. Innocence is a knowledge which means ignorance. The difference between this ignorance and moral ignorance is that the former is oriented in the direction of knowledge. With ignorance begins a knowledge the first characteristic of which is ignorance. This is the concept of bashfulness (shame). In bashfulness there is a dread because at the extremest expression of the difference composing the synthesis the spirit is determined in such a way that it is not merely qualified by relation to body but by relation to a body with the generic difference. Nevertheless bashfulness is surely a knowledge of the generic difference, but not as having relation to the generic difference, that is to say, the sexual impulse is not yet present as such. The real significance of bashfulness is that the spirit, so to speak, cannot recognize itself as the extreme point of the synthesis. For this reason the dread in bashfulness is so prodigiously ambiguous. There is not a trace of sensuous lust, and nevertheless there is a sense of shame. At what? At nothing.

And yet the individual may die of shame, and a wounded bashfulness is the deepest pain because it is the most inexplicable thing of all. Hence the dread in bashfulness can awaken by itself. But here of course it must be assumed that it is not lust which would like to play this role. An example of the latter may be found in a fairy tale by Fr. Schlegel (*Sämmtliche Werke*, Vol. 7, p. 15, in the story of Merlin).

In bashfulness the generic difference is posited, but not in relation to its other. This relation is brought about by the sexual impulse. But since this impulse is not an instinct, or not merely an instinct, it has *eo ipso* a τέλος [end or aim], which is propagation, whereas the state of repose is love, the pure erotic. All this while the spirit is not posited in this company. As soon as it is posited, not merely as constituting the synthesis, but as spirit, the erotic is at an end. Hence the highest pagan expression is that the erotic is the comical. This of course must not be taken in the sense in which a voluptuary can only mean that the erotic is comical and material for his lascivious wit; but it is the power and predominance of the intelligence which neutralizes in the indifference of the spirit both the erotic and the moral relation to it. This has a very deep reason. The dread in bashfulness consisted in the fact that the spirit felt itself foreign; now the spirit has completely conquered and views the sexual as the foreign and the comical. This freedom of the spirit bashfulness of course could not have. The sexual is the expression for the prodigious contradiction (*Wiederspruch*) that the immortal spirit is characterized as sex. This contradiction expresses itself in the deep shame which conceals this and does not dare to understand it. In the erotic experience this contradiction is understood as beauty, for beauty is precisely the unity of the psychical and the corporal. But this contradiction which the erotic explains by beauty is for the spirit at once beauty and the comical. Therefore the spirit's expression for the erotic is that it is at once beauty and the comical. Here there is no sensuous reflex cast upon the erotic, for that is sensuality, and in that case the individual lies far below the level of erotic beauty; but here we have the maturity of the spirit. Naturally, few men have understood this thought in its purity. Socrates did. Therefore when Xenophon represents him[10] as having said that one ought to love ugly women, this saying, like everything else by the help of Xenophon, became a disgusting and narrow-minded philistinism, which is least of all like Socrates. The meaning is that he had reduced the erotic to indifference; and the contradiction which underlies the comic he expressed correctly by the corresponding ironic contradiction that one should love the ugly.* Such a view, however, is very seldom presented in its lofty purity. For that there is needed a remarkable concordance of a fortunate historical development and a pristine talent. If there is any, even the most remote, animadversion possible, this view is disgusting and an affectation.

In Christianity the religious has suspended the erotic, not merely by an ethical misunderstanding of it as the sinful, but as the indifferent, because in spirit there is no difference between man and woman. Here the erotic is not ironically neutralized but suspended, because it is the tendency of Christianity to lead the spirit further. When in bashfulness the spirit is in dread and fear of arraying itself in the generic difference, the individual suddenly leaps away, and instead of penetrating it ethically grasps an explanation drawn from the highest sphere of spirit. This is one side of the monastic

---

* In this way must be understood what Socrates said to Critobulus about the kiss.[11] I believe it must be obvious to everyone that Socrates could not in seriousness talk so pathetically about the danger of the kiss, and also that he was not a ninny who did not dare to look at a woman. It is true that in southern lands and among more passionate peoples the kiss means something more than here in the north (about which subject one can consult a letter of Puteanus to John. Bapt. Saccum: *nesciunt nostrae virgines ullum libidinis rudimentum oculis aut osculis inesse, ideoque fruuntur. Vestrae sciunt.*[12] Cf. Kempius, *Dissertatio de osculis*, in Bayle's *Lexicon*), but nevertheless it is not like Socrates, either as an ironist or as a moralist, to talk in this way. As a matter of fact, when one assumes too lofty a tone as a moralist, one awakens desire and tempts the pupil almost against his will to become ironical against the teacher. Socrates' relation to Aspasia shows the same thing. He conversed with her without being at all concerned about the ambiguous life she led. He wanted only to learn from her (Athenaeus[13]), and as a teacher she seems to have had talent, for it is related[14] that husbands brought their wives with them to Aspasia merely that they might learn from her. On the other hand, as soon as Aspasia had wanted to make an impression upon him by her loveliness, Socrates presumably would have explained to her that one ought to love the ugly ones, and that she absolutely should not put her charms to any further strain, since to attain his purpose he had enough in Xantippe (cf. Xenophon's account of Socrates' view of his relation to Xantippe[15]).—Since unfortunately it occurs again and again that people go about the reading of everything with a preconceived opinion, it is no wonder that everybody has a definite notion that a Cynic is almost a dissolute man. Yet it might be possible precisely among the Cynics to find an example of that interpretation of the erotic as the comical.

view, whether that is more particularly characterized as ethical rigorism, or as a life in which contemplation is predominant.*

As dread is posited in bashfulness, so it is present in all erotic enjoyment (not by any means because it is sinful), and this is so even though the priest were to bless the couple ten times. Even when the erotic expresses itself as beautifully and purely and morally as possible, without being disturbed in its joy by any wanton reflection, dread is nevertheless present, not as a disturbing element, however, but as a concordant factor.

In this field it is very difficult to conduct observations. Here one must first of all take the precaution physicians take of never trying the pulse without making sure that they are not counting their own instead of that of the patient; so in this case one must take care that the movement one discovers is not the uneasiness of the observer in carrying out his observation. One thing, however, is sure, that in describing love, pure and innocent as they may represent it, all poets associate with it an element of dread. To pursue this subject more in detail is the business of an aestheticist. But why this dread? Because in the culmination of the erotic the spirit cannot take part. I will speak here with Greek candor. The spirit indeed is present, for it is this which constitutes the synthesis, but it cannot express itself in the erotic experience; it feels itself a stranger. It says as it were to the erotic, "My dear, I cannot be a third party here, therefore I will hide myself for the time being." But this precisely is dread, and also this precisely is bashfulness; for it is a great stupidity to suppose that the wedding ceremony of the Church, or the husband's fidelity in keeping himself unto her alone, is enough. Many a marriage has been profaned, and that not by an outsider. But when the erotic is pure and innocent and beautiful, the dread is friendly and mild, and therefore the poets are right in speaking about the sweet uneasiness. It is a matter of course, however, that the dread is greater on the part of woman.

Let us now return to the subject with which we were dealing above, the consequence for the individual of the fact of generation, which is the common "more" which every individual has in contrast with Adam. At the instant of conception the spirit is far

---

* However strange it may appear to one who is not accustomed to regard phenomena boldly, there is nevertheless a perfect analogy between Socrates' ironical interpretation of the erotic as the comical, and the relation of a monk to *mulieres subintroductae*. The abuse occurs of course only in the case of those who have a taste for the abuse.

away, and therefore the dread is greatest. In this dread the new individual comes into existence. At the instant of birth dread culminates a second time in woman, and at this instant the new individual comes into the world. That a woman in childbirth has dread is well known. Physiology has its explanation, psychology must also have its own. In childbirth woman is again at the utmost point of one extreme of the synthesis, hence the spirit trembles, for at this instant, when there is nothing for it to do, it is as it were suspended. Dread, however, is an expression for the perfection of human nature, and it is therefore only among the lesser kinds one finds analogies to the easy delivery of the beasts.

But the more dread, the more sensuousness. The procreated individual is more sensual than the original, and this "more" is the usual "more" which the fact of generation entails for every later individual in relation to Adam.

But the more of dread and sensuousness which every later individual has in comparison with Adam may of course in the particular individual signify a more or a less. This is the ground of the differences which in truth are so terrible that surely no one ventures to think of them in a deeper sense, that is, with genuine human sympathy, unless with a firmness which nothing can shake he is convinced that never is there found in this world, nor ever shall be found, such a "more" that by a simple transition it transforms the quantitative into the qualitative. What the Scripture teaches, that God visits the sins of the fathers upon the children unto the third and fourth generation, life itself proclaims in a loud enough voice. To want to chatter oneself away from this terrible fact by the explanation that this saying is a Jewish doctrine is of no avail. Christianity has never subscribed to the notion that every particular individual is in an outward sense privileged to begin from scratch. Every individual begins in a historical nexus, and the consequences of natural law are still as valid as ever. The difference now consists only in this, that Christianity teaches us to lift ourselves above that "more," and condemns him who does not do so as not willing to do so.

Precisely because sensuousness is here defined as a "more," the dread of the spirit in assuming responsibility for this "more" becomes a greater dread. There is implied here as a maximum the terrible fact that *dread of sin produces sin*. If one represents that evil desires, concupiscence, etc., are innate in the individual, one does not get the ambiguity in which the individual becomes both guilty and innocent. In the impotence of dread the individual succumbs, but precisely for this reason he is both guilty and innocent.

I will not adduce detailed examples of this infinitely fluctuating more and less. If such examples are to have any significance, they demand a vast aesthetic-psychological treatment.

B. CONSEQUENCE OF THE HISTORICAL SITUATION

If here I had to express in a single sentence the meaning of that "more" which characterizes every later individual in comparison with Adam, I would say: It consists in the fact that sensuousness may signify sin, that is, it may signify that obscure knowledge of sin which we have, as well as an obscure knowledge of what sin may signify in a broader reference, along with a misunderstood historical application of the historical refrain, *De te fabula narretur*, whereby the point, the originality of the individual, is left out, and the individual simply confounds himself with the race and its history. We do not say that sensuousness is sinfulness, but that sin makes it sinful. If now we picture to ourselves the later individual, we see that everyone has a historical environment in which it may eventuate that the sensuous may signify sin. For the individual himself it does not have this significance, but this general knowledge bestows upon dread a "more." The spirit then is placed not only in relation to the contradiction of sensuousness, but to that of sinfulness. It goes without saying that the innocent individual does not yet understand this knowledge, for it is only to be understood qualitatively, but nevertheless this knowledge is again a new possibility,. of such a sort that freedom, related in its possibility to the sensuous, falls into even greater dread.

That this common "more" may for the particular individual signify a more or a less, goes without saying. For example, to call attention at once to a difference of immense importance, after Christianity had come into the world and redemption was posited, sensuousness was seen in a new light, the light of contradiction, as it was not seen in paganism; and this serves precisely to confirm the proposition that sensuousness is sinfulness.

Within the Christian difference this "more" may again signify a more and a less. This is due to the relation of each particular innocent individual to his environment. In this respect the most diverse causes may produce the same effect. The possibility of freedom announces itself in dread. An admonition may now cause the individual to succumb in dread (it is to be remembered that I am constantly speaking psychologically and never annul the qualitative leap), and this in spite of the fact that the admonition was of course meant to produce the opposite effect. The sight of the sinful may save one individual and hurl down another. A jest may have the same effect as seriousness, and vice versa. Speech and silence may produce an effect which is the opposite to that which was intended. To this there are no limits, and hence one perceives here again the correctness of the definition, that this is a quantitative more and less; for the quantitative is precisely the infinite limit.

I will not carry out here any further this experimenting observation, for it delays us. Life, however, is rich enough in examples, if only one understands how to see; one need not journey to Paris and London—and that is of no avail when one cannot see.

Moreover, dread has here again the same ambiguity it always has. At this point a maximum may be reached which corresponds to that mentioned above, when it was said that the individual in dread of sin produces sin. Here the formula is: *The individual in dread, not of becoming guilty, but of being regarded as guilty, becomes guilty.*

Moreover, the utmost "more" in this direction is, that this individual from his earliest awaking is so placed and influenced that for him sensuousness has become identical with sin, and this utmost "more" will appear in the most painful form of collisions, when in the whole surrounding world he finds absolutely nothing that affords him support. If to this extremest "more" is added the confusion that the individual confounds himself with his historical knowledge of sin, and in the pallor of dread subsumes himself *qua* individual under the same category, forgetting the category of freedom which says: "If thou doest likewise"—then the very extremest "more" is reached.

What has here been so briefly suggested that it requires a pretty rich experience to understand that much has been said, and said definitely and clearly, is commonly spoken of as the power of example. Undeniably (though not precisely in these superphilosophical times) a great deal has been very well said about this subject; but often there is lacking the psychological middle term which explains how it is that the example produces an effect. In this sphere moreover they have sometimes treated the matter a little too carelessly and have not noticed that a single little mistake is capable of throwing life's prodigious balance sheet into confusion. The attention of psychology is fixed exclusively upon particulars and has not at the same time ready at hand its eternal categories, and is not circumspect enough when saving mankind to save each individual of the race, cost what it may. Example is supposed to have had its effect upon the child. The child is represented as a regular little angel, but the depraved environment cast it into perdition. One keeps on relating and relating how bad the environment was—and so, and so the child became depraved. But if this comes about by a simple quantitative process, every concept is annulled. This fact is not noticed. Or the child is represented as so fundamentally wicked that the good example can do it no good. But take heed that this child does not become so wicked that it acquires the power not merely to make fools of its parents but of all human speech and thought, just as a *rana paradoxa*[16] mocks and defies the naturalist's classification of frogs. There are many men who understand, to be sure, how to look at the particular, but are not capable of having at the same time the totality *in mente*; but every such way of looking at things, though in other respects it is meritorious, can only occasion confusion.—Or the child was, as most children are, neither good nor bad, but then it fell into good company and became good, or into bad company and became bad. But the middle terms! the middle terms! Let someone introduce a middle term which has the ambiguity that it rescues the thought (without which indeed the child's salvation is an illusion) that the child, in whatever "how" it was, can become both guilty and innocent. If one has not the middle term at hand promptly and clearly, then the concepts of original sin, of sin, of the race, of the individual, are lost, and the child along with them.

Sensuousness then is not sinfulness, but by the fact that sin was posited, and by the fact that it continues to be posited, sensuousness becomes sinful. It goes without saying that sinfulness now signifies something else, but we have nothing to do here with what else it may signify where properly we are employed in scrutinizing psychologically the state which precedes sin and which, psychologically speaking, predisposes to sin more or less.

By eating the fruit of knowledge the distinction between good and evil came into the world, but with that also the sexual distinction as a propensity. No science can explain how. Psychology comes nearest to doing so and explains the last step in the approximation, which is freedom's apparition before itself in the dread of possibility, or in the nothingness of possibility, or in the nothing of dread. If the object of dread is a something, then there is no leap, but a quantitative transition. The later individual has a "more" in comparison with Adam, and again a more or a less in comparison with other men, but nevertheless it holds good that the object of dread is a nothing. If its object is a something of such a sort that viewed essentially, i.e. in relation to freedom, it signifies something, there is no leap, but only a quantitative transition which confuses every concept. Even when I say that for an individual before he makes the leap sensuousness is posited as sinfulness, it holds good nevertheless that it is not essentially posited as such, for essentially he does not posit it nor understand it. Even when I say that in the procreated individual there is posited a "more" of sensuousness, nevertheless this "more" is, so far as the leap is concerned, an invalid "more."

If science has any other psychological middle term which dogmatically, ethically and psychologically possesses the advantage dread has, then one is free to prefer it.

Moreover, it is easy to see that what has been expounded can perfectly well be brought into accord with the explanation commonly given of sin as selfishness or egoism. But when one is absorbed in this definition, one does not undertake at all to explain the precedent psychological difficulty; and moreover this defines sin too pneumatically, not paying sufficient attention to the fact that sin by being posited posits sensuousness just as much as it does a spiritual consequence.

Seeing that in modern philosophy[17] sin has so often been explained as egoism, it is incomprehensible that no one has perceived that precisely in this consists the impossibility of finding a place for sin in any science. For the egoistic is precisely the particular (*Enkelte*), and only the particular individual can know it, as a particular individual, since when viewed under general categories it can signify everything, in such wise that this everything signifies nothing at all. Therefore the definition of sin as egoism may be quite correct, precisely when at the same time one holds fast the fact that, scientifically speaking, it is so empty of content that it means nothing at all. Finally, in this definition, that sin is selfishness, no account is taken of the distinction between sin and original sin, nor of the sense in which one explains the other, sin explaining original sin, and original sin explaining sin.

As soon as one begins to talk scientifically about this egoism, everything is dissolved into tautology, or else one resorts to *esprit*, whereby everything is brought to confusion. Who can forget that natural philosophy has found this egoism in the whole creation, found it in the movement of the stars, which nevertheless are bound to obedience under the law of the universe? They have found that the centrifugal force in nature is egoism. When a concept has been carried so far, it may well go to bed, in order if possible to sleep off its drunkenness and become sober again. Here our age has been indefatigable in getting everything to signify all things. We have seen how briskly and pertinaciously some *spirituel* mystagogue[18] or another will prostitute a whole mythology in order by his falcon eye to make every single myth a fantasy for his jew's-harp. Sometimes one sees a whole Christian terminology brought to degeneration and perdition by the ostentatious use one speculator or another makes of it.

If one does not first make clear to oneself what "self" means, there is not much use in saying of sin that it is selfishness. But "self" signifies precisely the contradiction of positing the general as the particular (*Enkelte*). Only when the concept of the particular individual (*Enkelte*) is given can there be any question of the selfish. But although there have lived countless millions of such "selves," no science can state what the self is, without stating it in perfectly general terms.* And this is the wonderful thing about life, that every man who gives heed to himself knows what no science knows, since he knows what he himself is; and this is the profundity of the Greek saying, γνῶθι σεαυτόν (know thyself),†

---

* It is worth while reflecting upon this, for precisely at this point it must become evident to what extent the new principle that thought and being are one is adequate, when we do not spoil it by misunderstandings which are inept and in part stupid, but on the other hand do not wish to have a highest principle which involves us in thoughtlessness. The general *is* only by the fact that it is thought or can be thought (not only in imaginary experiments—for what all cannot a man think!) and is *as* that which can be thought. The point in the particular is its negative, its repellent relationship to the general; but as soon as this is thought away, individuality is annulled, and as soon as it is thought it is transformed in such a way that either one does not think it but only imagines one is thinking it, or does think it and only imagines that it is included in the process of thought.

† The Latin saying, *unum noris omnes* [if you know one, you know all], expresses light-mindedly the same thing, and expresses it really if by *unum* one

which so long has been understood in the German way[19] as pure self-consciousness, the airiness of idealism. Surely it is high time to try to understand it in the Greek way, and then again in such a way as the Greeks would have understood it if they had had Christian presuppositions. But the real "self" is first posited by the qualitative leap. In the situation preceding this there can be no question of such a thing. Therefore when one would explain sin by selfishness, one becomes involved in confusions, since on the contrary it is true that by sin and in sin selfishness comes into being. If it were to be said that selfishness was the occasion of Adam's sin, then this explanation is a game in which the interpreter finds what he himself had first hidden. If it were to be said that selfishness was the cause of Adam's sin, then the intervening state has been leapt over and the interpretation has been accomplished with suspicious ease. Moreover, in this way one learns nothing about the significance of the sexual. Here I am back again at the old point. The sexual is not sinfulness, but (if for an instant I may speak by way of "accommodation" and speak foolishly) supposing Adam had not sinned, then the sexual would never have been posited as a propensity. A perfect spirit cannot be conceived as sexually differentiated. This is in harmony with the doctrine of the Church concerning the character of the resurrection,[20] in harmony with its notion of angels,[21] in harmony with the dogmatic definitions of the person of Christ. Just as a suggestion I note that whereas Christ was subjected to all human trials, there is nothing said of any temptation in this respect, which may be explained precisely by the consideration that he withstood all temptations.

Sensuousness is not sinfulness. Sensuousness in the state of innocence is not sinfulness, and yet sensuousness is present, Adam indeed was in need of food and drink, etc. The generic difference is posited in innocence but is not posited as such. Only at the instant when sin is posited is the generic difference also posited as propensity [*Drift*].

Here as usual I must deprecate every mistaken conclusion, as if, for example, it now ought to be the true task to ignore the sensual, i.e. in an external sense to reduce it to naught. Once the sexual

understands the thinker himself, and then does not inquisitively go scouting after the *omnes*, but seriously holds fast to this one, which really is all. Generally men do not believe this, and they even think that it is too proud. Surely the reason is that they are too cowardly and indolent to venture to understand and to earn the understanding of true pride.

is posited as the extreme point of the synthesis, it is no use ignoring it. The task is of course to win it into conformity with the destiny of the spirit. (Here lie all the moral problems of the erotic.) The realization of this task is the triumph of love in a man in whom the spirit has triumphed in such a way that the sexual is forgotten and only remembered in forgetfulness. When this has come about, then sensuousness is transfigured into spirit and dread driven out.

If now one will compare this view (call it Christian or what you will) with the Greek view, I believe that more has been won than has been lost. True, there has indeed been lost something of that melancholy erotic *Heiterkeit*,[22] but there has also been gained a spiritual quality unknown to Hellenism. The only men who truly lose are the many who go on living continually as if it were 6000 years ago sin came into the world, as if it were a curiosity which did not concern them. For they do not win the Greek *Heiterkeit*, which is precisely a thing which cannot be *won*, but only lose it, nor do they win the eternal meed of spirit.

CHAPTER III

Dread as the Consequence of that Sin which is the Default of the Consciousness of Sin

IN THE foregoing chapters it was constantly affirmed that man is a synthesis of soul and body which is' constituted and sustained by spirit. Dread—to use a term which says the same thing that was said in the foregoing discussion but points forward to what is to follow—dread was the instant in the individual life.

There is a category which is constantly used in modern philosophy—no less in logic than in historico-philosophical investigations—and that is "transition." What it means more precisely we are never told. It is employed without more ado, and while Hegel and the Hegelian School startle the world by the mighty thought of the presuppositionless beginning of philosophy, or that nothing must precede philosophy but the most complete absence of presuppositions, no embarrassment is felt in employing the terms "transition," "negation" and "mediation," i.e. the principles of movement in Hegelian thought, in such a way that no place is definitely assigned to them in the systematic progression. If this is not a presupposition, I do not know what a presupposition is; for to employ something which is nowhere explained is in effect to presuppose it. One might think that the System must have such marvelous transparency and introspectiveness that like the omphalopscychoi[1] it would gaze immovably at the central Nothing for so long a time that everything would explain itself and its whole content would of its own accord come into existence. This openness to public inspection the System surely must have. Such, however, is not the case, and the Systematic thought seems to be vowed to secretiveness with respect to its inmost motions and emotions. Negation, transition, mediation, are three masked men of suspicious appearance, the secret agents (*agentia*), which provoke all movements. Hegel would hardly call them "hot heads," for it is by his sovereign permission they carry on their game so brazenly that even in logic terms and expressions are employed which are drawn from the observation of transition in time: "thereupon," "when," "this is like being," "this is like becoming."

But let that be as it will, and let logic tend to its own affairs.

The word "transition" cannot be anything but a witty conceit in logic. It belongs in the sphere of historical freedom, for transition is a *state*, and it is actual.* Plato clearly enough perceived the difficulty of introducing transition into pure metaphysics, and for this reason the category of "the instant"† cost him so much effort.

* Therefore when Aristotle says that the transition from possibility to actuality is a κίνησις, this is not to be understood logically but with reference to the historical freedom.

† By Plato the instant was conceived in a purely abstract way. To orient oneself in its dialectic one must take into account the fact that the instant is non-being under the category of time. Non-being (τὸ μὴ ὄν; τὸ κενόν, of the Pythagoreans) preoccupied the ancient philosophers much more than it does the modern ones. Non-being was conceived ontologically by the Eleatic philosophers, to the effect that what is affirmed about it can only be affirmed in contradictions, that only being *is*. If one would follow this further, one will see that it recurs in all spheres. In metaphysical propaedeutics the proposition is expressed thus: He who affirms non-being says nothing at all. (This misunderstanding was combatted in the *Sophist*, and in a more mimic way it was combatted already in an earlier work, *Gorgias*). Finally, in the practical spheres the Sophists made use of non-being in such a way that they annulled all moral concepts: non-being *is* not, *ergo* everything is true, *ergo* everything is good, *ergo* a deceit, etc., does not exist. Socrates combats this in several dialogues. Plato, however, dealt with it principally in the *Sophist*, which, like all Plato's dialogues, elucidates at the same time by art the doctrine it teaches formally; for the Sophist, whose definition and concept the dialogue is seeking to discover while it follows its principal theme of non-being, is himself a non-being, and thus both the concept and this example of it come into existence at the same time in the course of the argument in which the Sophist is attacked and which ends with his not being annihilated but brought into existence, which was the worst thing that could befall him, seeing that in spite of his sophistic which, like the armor of Mars, is able to make him invisible, he must come out openly. Modern philosophy has not yet got any further in the apprehension of non-being, in spite of its pretense to be Christian. Greek philosophy and modern philosophy alike take the position that everything depends upon getting non-being to come into existence; for to do away with it and cause it to vanish seems to them too easy. The Christian view takes the position that non-being is everywhere present as the Nothing out of which all is created, as appearance and vanity, as sin, as sensuousness divorced from the spirit, as the temporal forgotten by eternity; wherefore the whole point is to do away with it and get being in its stead. Only with this orientation does the concept of atonement receive an historically correct interpretation, in the sense in which Christianity brought it into the world. If the interpretation is carried out in the opposite sense (the starting point of the movement being derived from the conception that non-being does not exist), then the Atonement is volatilized and turned inside out.—It is in *Parmenides* Plato propounds "the instant." This dialogue is engaged in showing the contradiction within the concepts themselves, and Socrates expresses this with such precision that it does not exactly redound to the discredit of that beautiful old Greek philosophy, but may well serve to put to shame a new and boastful philosophy which does not make, like the Greek, great demands upon itself, but upon men and their admiration. Socrates remarks that it would not be wonderful if a man were able to demonstrate the contradictoriness (τὸ ἐναντίον)

To ignore the difficulty is certainly not to "go further" than Plato; to ignore it by a pious fraud against thought in order to get speculation afloat and start movement agoing is to treat speculation as a rather finite affair. I remember, however, once hearing a speculator say[2] that one ought not to think too much about difficulties beforehand, for with that one would never get to the point of

involved in a particular thing which is made up of diversities, but if one were able to show the contradiction in the concepts themselves, that would be something to wonder at (ἀλλ' εἰ ὅ ἐστιν ἕν, αὐτό τοῦτο πολλά ἀποδείξει καί αὖ τά πολλά δή ἕν, τοῦτο ἤδη θαυμάσομαι. καί περί τῶν ἄλλων ἀπάντων ὡσαύτως. §129 B.C.). The method as usual is that of experimental dialectics. It is assumed that unity (τό ἕν) is and is not, and then it is shown what the consequence will be for it and for the rest. The instant appears now to be that strange being (ἄτοπον—the Greek word is admirably chosen) which lies between movement and repose, without occupying any time; and to this and out of this "the moving" passes over into rest, and "the reposing" into movement. The instant therefore becomes the general category of transition (μεταβολή); for Plato shows that the instant is related in the same way to the transition from unity to plurality and from plurality to unity, from likeness to unlikeness, etc., it is the instant in which there is neither ἕν nor πολλά, neither discrimination nor integration (οὔτι διακρίνεται οὔτι ξυγκρίνεται, §157,A). Now with all this Plato has the merit of making the difficulty clear, but nevertheless the instant remains a mute atomistic abstraction, which is not any further explained when one ignores it. Now if logic is willing to affirm that there is no transition in it (and if it has this category, it surely must have its place assigned to it in the System, seeing that in fact it is already operative there), then it will become clearer that the historical sphere and all the knowledge which reposes upon a historical presupposition has the category of the instant. This category is of great importance as a barrier against the philosophy of paganism and the equally pagan philosophy in Christianity. Another passage in the dialogue *Parmenides* makes evident the consequence of the fact that the instant is such an abstraction [in Plato's conception of it]. It is shown then how under the category of time there emerges the contradiction that unity (τό ἕν) becomes younger and older than itself and than plurality (τά πολλά), and then in turn, that it is neither younger nor older than itself and plurality (§151,E). Unity nevertheless must exist; it is said, and now it is defined thus: participation in a being or an essence in the present (τό δέ εἶναι ἄλλο τί ἐστι ἤ μέθεξις οὐσίας μετά χρόνου τοῦ παρόντος §151,E). In the further development of the contradiction it then appears that the present (τό νῦν) wavers between meaning the present, the eternal, the instant. This "now" (τό νῦν) lies between "was" and "will be," and unity, as it strives forward from the past to the future, cannot leap by this "now." So then it comes to a stop with the "now," does not become older but is older. In modern philosophy the abstraction culminates in "pure being"; but pure being is the most abstract expression for eternity, and in turn, like "nothing," it is the instant. Here it is evident again how important "the instant" is, because only by this category can one succeed in giving eternity its proper significance. Eternity and the instant are the extreme terms of the contradiction, whereas otherwise conceived the dialectical witchcraft makes eternity and the instant signify the same thing. It is only with Christianity that the sensuous, the temporal, the instant, are to be understood, precisely because it is only with it the eternal becomes essential.

speculating. If the important thing is merely to begin to speculate, and not that one's speculation might really become speculation, then it was said with a fine spirit of resolution that one must merely try to get to the point of speculating, just as it would be laudable in a man who had not the means to drive to the Deer Park[3] in his own carriage to say, "One ought not to be troubled by such things, one can quite well ride in the charabanc.[4]" Quite true. It is to be hoped that both conveyances will reach the Deer Park. On the other hand, that man will hardly reach speculation who was so firmly resolved not to trouble himself about the mode of conveyance, if only he could barely get to the point of speculating.

In the sphere of historical freedom transition is a state. However, in order to understand this affirmation one must not forget that the new situation comes about by the leap. For if this is not kept in mind, transition acquires a quantitative preponderance over the elasticity of the leap.

So then, man was said to be a synthesis of soul and body; but he is at the same time *a synthesis of the temporal and the eternal.* I have no objection to recognizing that this has often been said; I have no wish to discover novelties, but rather it is my joy and my darling occupation to think upon things which seem perfectly simple.

As for the latter synthesis, it evidently is not fashioned in the same way as the former. In the former case the two factors were soul and body, and the spirit was a third term, but was a third term in such a sense that there could not properly be any question of a synthesis until the spirit was posited. The other synthesis has only two factors: the temporal and the eternal. Where is the third term? And if there be no third term, there is really no synthesis; for a synthesis of that which is a contradiction cannot be completed as a synthesis without a third term, for the recognition that the synthesis is a contradiction is precisely the assertion that it is not a synthesis. What then is the temporal?

When time is correctly defined as infinite succession, it seems plausible to define it also as the present, the past and the future. However this distinction is incorrect, if one means by it that this is implied in time itself; for it first emerges with the relation of time to eternity and the reflection of eternity in it. If in the infinite succession of time one could in fact find a foothold, i.e. a present, which would serve as a dividing point, then this division would be quite correct. But precisely because every moment, like the sum of the moments, is a process (a going-by) no moment is a present, and in the same sense there is neither past, present, nor future. If one thinks it possible to maintain this division, it is because we *spatialize* a moment, but thereby the infinite succession is brought to a standstill, and that is because one introduces a visual representation, visualizing time instead of thinking it. But even so it is not correctly thought, for even in this visual representation the infinite succession of time is a present infinitely void of content. (This is the parody of the eternal.) The Hindus speak of a line of kings which has reigned for 70,000 years.[5] About the kings nothing is known, not even their names (as I assume). Taking this as an illustration of time, these 70,000 years are for thought an infinite vanishing; for visual representation they widen out spatially into an illusive view of a nothing infinitely void.* On the other hand, so soon as we let one moment succeed the other we posit the present.

The present, however, is not the concept of time, unless precisely as something infinitely void, which again is precisely the infinite vanishing. If one does not give heed to this, then, however swiftly one may let it pass, one has nevertheless posited the present, and having posited that, one lets it appear again in the definition of the past and the future.

On the contrary, the eternal is the present. For thought, the eternal is the present as an annulled [*aufgehoben*] succession (time was succession, going by). For visual representation, eternity is a going-forth, yet it never budges from the spot, because for visual representation it is a present infinitely rich in content. Likewise in the eternal there is not to be found any division of the past and the future, because the present is posited as the annulled succession.

So time is infinite succession. The life which is in time and is merely that of time has no present. It is true that to characterize the sensuous life it is commonly said that it is "in the instant" and only in the instant. The instant is here understood as something abstracted from the eternal, and if this is to be accounted the present, it is a parody of it. The present is the eternal, or rather the

---

* Moreover, this is space. Just here the practiced reader will see the proof that my representation is right, since for abstract thinking time and space are absolutely identical (*nacheinander* and *nebeneinander*), and they become so for visual representation, and so it is with the definition of God as omnipresent.

eternal is the present, and the present is full. In this sense the Roman said of the Deity that He is *praesens (praesentes dii)*, and in using this expression for the Deity His powerful aid was indicated at the same time.

The instant characterizes the present as having no past and no future, for in this precisely consists the imperfection of the sensuous life. The eternal also characterizes the present as having no past and no future, and this is the perfection of the eternal.

If one would now employ the instant to define time, and let the instant indicate the purely abstract exclusion of the past and the future, and by the same token of the present also, then the instant precisely is not the present, for that which in purely abstract thinking lies between the past and the future has no existence at all. But one sees from this that the instant is not a mere characterization of time, for what characterizes time is only that it goes by, and hence time, if it is to be defined by any of the characteristics revealed in time itself, is the passed time. On the other hand, if time and eternity are to touch one another, it must be in time— and with this we have reached the instant.

"The instant" [in Danish, *Øjeblikket*—"a glance of the eye"] is a figurative expression, and for that reason not so easy to deal with. Yet it is a pretty word to reflect upon. Nothing is so swift as a glance of the eye, and yet it is commensurable with the content and value of eternity. Thus when Ingeborg[6] gazes out over the sea to descry Frithiof, this is a picture of what the figurative word signifies. An outburst of her emotion, a sigh, a word, has, as a sound, more the character of time, as a thing that vanishes it is more like the present, and has not so much the presence of the eternal in it, and for this reason a sigh, a word, etc., has power to help the soul to get rid of the weight which oppresses it, precisely because the oppression, if only it finds utterance, begins already to become a past. A glance is therefore a designation of time, but note that this means, of time in the fateful conflict when it is touched by eternity.* What we call "the instant," Plato calls $\dot{\epsilon}\xi$-$\alpha\acute{\iota}\phi\nu\eta\varsigma$ ["the sudden"]. However it may be explained etymologi-

---

* It is noteworthy that Greek art culminates in statuary, in which it is precisely the glance that is lacking. This, however, has its deep reason in the fact that the Greeks did not in the profounder sense comprehend the concept of spirit, and therefore did not in the profoundest sense comprehend the sensuous and the temporal. How striking is the contrast that in Christianity God is pictorially represented as an eye!

cally, it is related at all events to the notion of invisibility, because by the Greeks time and eternity alike were conceived abstractly, since the Greeks lacked the concept of the temporal owing to the fact that they lacked the concept of spirit. In Latin it is called *momentum*, which by derivation (from *movere*) merely expresses the vanishing of time.*

Thus understood, the instant is not properly an atom of time but an atom of eternity. It is the first reflection of eternity in time, its first effort as it were to bring time to a stop. For this reason Hellenism did not understand the instant; for even if it comprehended the atom of eternity, it did not comprehend that it was the instant, did not define it with a forward orientation but with a backward, since for Hellenism the atom of eternity was essentially eternity, and so neither time nor eternity had true justice done it.

The synthesis of the eternal and the temporal is not a second synthesis but is the expression for the first synthesis in consequence of which man is a synthesis of soul and body sustained by spirit. No sooner is the spirit posited than the instant is there. For this reason it can be said reproachfully of man that he lives only in the instant, since this comes about by an arbitrary abstraction. Nature does not lie in the instant.

As it is with the sensuous, so it is also with the temporal; for the temporal seems even more imperfect, and the instant still more insignificant, than the apparently secure persistence of nature in

* In the New Testament there is a poetical paraphrase of the instant. Paul says that the world will pass away "in an instant, in the twinkling of an eye" (ἐν ἀτόμῳ καὶ ἐν ῥιπῇ ὀφθαλμοῦ). By that he also expresses the thought that the instant is commensurable with eternity, because the instant of destruction expresses at the same instant eternity. Allow me to illustrate what I mean, and forgive me if there is found anything offensive in the parable I employ. Here in Copenhagen there once upon a time were two actors, who perhaps hardly reflected that a deeper significance might be found in their performance. They came on the stage, placed themselves opposite one another, and then began a pantomime representation of some passionate conflict. When the pantomimic play was in full swing, and the spectators were following the play with keen expectancy of what was to come after, the actors suddenly came to a stop and remained motionless, as though they were petrified in the pantomimic expression of the instant. This may produce a most comical effect, because the instant becomes accidentally commensurable with the eternal. The effect of sculpture is due to the fact that the eternal expression is expressed eternally; the comic effect, on the other hand, by the fact that the accidental expression was eternalized.

time. And yet it is exactly the converse, for nature's security is due to the fact that time has no significance for it. Only in the instant does history begin. Man's sensuousness is by sin posited as sinfulness, and therefore is lower than that of the beast, and yet this is because here the higher life begins, for now begins spirit.

The instant is that ambiguous moment in which time and eternity touch one another, thereby positing *the temporal*, where time is constantly intersecting eternity and eternity constantly permeating time. Only now does that division we talked about acquire significance: the present, the past, and the future.

In making this division, attention is at once drawn to the fact that in a certain sense the future signifies more than the present and the past; for the future is in a sense the whole of which the past is a part, and in a sense the future may signify the whole. This is due to the fact that the eternal means first of all the future, or that the future is the incognito in which the eternal, as incommensurable for time, would nevertheless maintain its relations with time. Thus we sometimes speak of the future as identical with eternity: the future life = eternal life. Since the Greeks did not have in a deeper sense the concept of the eternal, neither did they have the concept of the future. One cannot therefore reproach the Greek life for losing itself in the instant, or rather we cannot even say that it was lost; for by the Greeks the temporal was conceived just as naïvely as was the sensuous, because the category of spirit was lacking.

The instant and the future posit in turn the past. If the Greek life might be supposed to define time in any sense, it is as time past, yet without defining this by its relation to the present and the future, but defining it, like the definition of time in general, as a going-by. Here the significance of the Platonic recollection[7] is evident. The Greek eternity lies behind, as the past into which one enters only backwards.* However, to say that eternity is the past is to present a perfectly abstract concept of it, whether this be further defined philosophically (by the philosophical dying to the world)[8] or historically.[9]

In general, by seeing how the past, the future, the eternal are defined, one can see how the instant has been defined. If there is no instant, then the eternal appears to be behind, like the past. It is

---

* Here again one must bear in mind the category I maintain, i.e. repetition, by which one enters eternity forwards.

as though I were to picture a man walking along a road but do not assume that he takes a step, then the road behind him appears to be the distance traveled. If the instant is posited, but merely as a *discrimen*, then the future is the eternal. If the instant is posited, so is the eternal—but also the future, which comes again like the past. This appears clearly in the Greek, the Jewish, and the Christian conceptions. The concept around which everything turns in Christianity, the concept which makes all things new, is the fullness of time, is the instant as eternity, and yet this eternity is at once the future and the past. If one does not give heed to this, one cannot save any concept from heretical and treasonable admixtures which destroy the concept. One does not get the past as a thing for itself but in simple continuity with the future—and with that the concepts of conversion, atonement, redemption, are resolved in the significance of world-history, and resolved in the individual historical development. One does not get the future as a thing for itself but in simple continuity with the present—and with that the concepts of resurrection and judgment come to naught.

Let us now picture to ourselves Adam, and then remember that every subsequent individual begins exactly the same way, only within the quantitative difference which is the consequence of the fact of generation and of the historical situation. For Adam then, just as much as for every subsequent individual, there is the instant. The synthesis of the soulish and the bodily is to be posited by spirit, but the spirit is the eternal, and therefore this is accomplished only when the spirit posits at the same time along with this the second synthesis of the eternal and the temporal. So long as the eternal is not posited, the instant *is* not, or is only as a *discrimen*. Therefore, seeing that in the state of innocence the spirit is characterized merely as a dreaming spirit, the eternal manifests itself as the future, for this, as I have said, is the first expression of the eternal, is its incognito. Just as in the foregoing chapter the spirit when it was about to be posited in the synthesis or rather was about to posit the synthesis, as the spirit's (freedom's) possibility in the individual, expressed itself as dread, so here in turn the future, the possibility of the eternal (i.e. of freedom) in the individual is dread. When then the possibility of freedom manifests itself before freedom, freedom succumbs, and the temporal now emerges in the same way as did sensuousness with the significance of sinfulness. Here again I say that this is the last psychological approximation to the qualitative leap. The difference between Adam and the subsequent individual is that by the latter the future is conceived more reflectively than by Adam. Psychologically speaking, this "more" may have a terrible significance, but in relation to the qualitative leap its significance is unessential. The highest maximum of difference in comparison with Adam is that the future seems to be anticipated by the past, or, in other words, it is the dread that possibility has been lost before it has been lost.

The possible corresponds precisely to the future. For freedom the possible is the future; and for time the future is the possible. Corresponding to both of these in the individual life is dread. A precise and correct linguistic usage associates therefore dread and the future. It is true that one is sometimes said to be in dread of the past, and this seems to be a contradiction. Nevertheless, upon closer inspection it appears that this manner of speaking points in one way or another to the future. The past of which I am supposed to be in dread must stand in a relation of possibility to me. If I am in dread of a past misfortune, this is not in so far as it is past, but in so far as it may be repeated, i.e. become future. If I am in dread of a past fault, it is because I have not put it in an essential relation to myself as past, and have in some way or another prevented it from being past. For in case it is really past, I cannot be in dread but only repentant. If I do not repent, then I have first taken the liberty of making my relation to it dialectical, but thereby the fault itself has become a possibility and not something completely passed. If I am in dread of punishment, it is only when this is put in a dialectical relation with the fault (otherwise I bear my punishment), and then I am in dread of the possible and the future.

So again we have reached the point where we were in Chapter I. Dread is the psychological state which precedes sin, comes as near as possible to it, and is as provocative as possible of dread, but without explaining sin, which breaks forth first in the qualitative leap.

The instant sin is posited, the temporal is sin.* We do not say

* From the characterization of the temporal as sinfulness death in turn follows as punishment. This is a progression, an analogy of which, *si placet*, may be found in the fact that, even in relation to the external phenomenon, death is more terrible in the degree that the organism is more perfect. Thus, whereas the death and decay of a plant diffuses an odor almost more delicious than its spicy breath, the decay of an animal, on the other hand, infects the air. It is true

that the temporal is sinfulness, any more than that the sensuous is sinfulness; but for the fact that sin is posited the temporal signifies sinfulness. Therefore that man sins who lives merely in the instant abstracted from the eternal. If Adam (to speak again by way of "accommodation" and to speak foolishly) had not sinned, he would the same instant have passed over into eternity. On the other hand, so soon as sin is posited it does not avail to want to abstract oneself from the temporal, any more than it would from the sensuous.*

§ I

Dread owing to the default of spirit

LOOKING at life broadly, one will soon be convinced that even what has here been set forth is correct, viz. that dread is the last psychological state out of which sin breaks forth with the qualitative leap, yet nevertheless the whole of paganism and its repetition within Christianity knows of nothing but quantitative differences from which the qualitative leap of sin does not break forth. This

in a deeper sense that the more highly we value man, the more terrible death appears. The beast cannot properly be said to die; but when the spirit is posited as spirit, death appears terrible. The dread of death therefore corresponds to that of childbirth, though with this I do not subscribe to what in part is said truly, in part only wittily, in part enthusiastically, in part lightly, about death being a metamorphosis. At the instant of death man finds himself at the extremest point of the synthesis; the spirit cannot, as it were, be present, and yet it must wait, for the body must die. The pagan view of death—as the pagan's sensuousness was more naïve and his sense of time more carefree—was milder and more attractive, but it lacked the highest element. Let one read the beautiful essay by Lessing[10] on the representation of death in classical art, and one cannot deny that one is put in a mood of pleasurable sadness by this picture of the sleeping genius, or by observing the beautiful solemnity with which the genius of death bows his head and extinguishes the torch. There is, if one will, something indescribably persuasive and alluring in the thought of trusting oneself to such a guide, who is as tranquilizing as a recollection in which nothing is recollected. But on the other hand there is in turn something uncanny in following this mute guide; for he conceals nothing, his form is no incognito, as he is, so is death, and therewith all is over. There is an unfathomable sadness in seeing this guide with his friendly figure bend over the dying man and with the breath of his last kiss extinguish the last spark of life, while all he has experienced has already vanished little by little, and death only is left, which, itself unexplained, explains that the whole of life was a game in which all, the greatest and the least, went out like tapers, one by one, and at last the soul itself. But then there is implied by it also the muteness of annihilation, because the whole thing was only a childish game, and now the game is finished.

* What has been set forth here might as well have found a place in Chapter I. However, I have chosen to put it here because it leads on to what is to follow.

situation, however, is not the situation of innocence, but, viewed from the standpoint of the spirit, it is precisely a situation of sinfulness.

It is remarkable that Christian orthodoxy has constantly taught that paganism lies in sin, whereas the consciousness of sin was nevertheless first posited by Christianity. Orthodoxy, however, is in the right, if it would explain itself a little more precisely. By quantitative definitions paganism, so to speak, procrastinates, never gets to sin in the deepest sense—but precisely this is sin.

It is easy to show that such is the case in paganism. In the case of paganism within Christianity the situation is different. The life of Christian paganism is neither guilty nor not guilty. Strictly speaking, it makes no distinction between present, past, future, eternal. Its life and its history go on like the writing in those old days when people used no marks of punctuation but crabbedly traced on the paper one word, one sentence, after another. Aesthetically regarded, this is very comical. For while it is pretty to hear a brook run through life with a purling sound, it is comical that a sum of rational creatures are transformed into a perpetual murmur without meaning. Whether philosophy can make use of this *plebs* as a category by employing it as a substratum for something greater, like the vegetative muddle which gradually becomes solid ground, first peat, and finally soil—that I do not know. Viewed from the standpoint of the spirit, such an existence is sin, and the least one can do for it is by declaring this fact to demand of it spirit.

What I have just said does not apply to paganism. Such an existence is only to be found within Christianity. The reason is that the more highly spirit is posited, the baser appears exclusion from it; and the more lofty the good that is lost, the more miserable in their base contentment are "those who have ceased to grieve" (the ἀπηλγηκότες, as Paul calls them in Ephesians 4:19). If one will compare the blissfulness of spirit-lessness with the condition of slaves in paganism, it will appear that after all there was some sense in slavery, for in itself it was nothing. On the other hand, to be lost in spirit-lessness is the most terrible thing of all; for precisely this is its misfortune, that it has a relation to spirit which proves not to be a relation. Spirit-lessness may therefore to a certain degree possess the whole content of spirit—not as spirit, be it noted, but as jest, galimatias, phrase, etc. It may possess truth—not as truth, be it noted, but as rumor and old wives' tales. Aesthetically viewed, this is the profoundly comical aspect of spirit-lessness, an aspect which is not generally noticed, because he who presents it on the stage or in fiction is himself more or less insecure when it comes to the question of spirit. Therefore in representing spirit-lessness one commonly puts into the mouth of the character sheer twaddle, for the reason that one has not the courage to attribute to the spirit-less man the same words one uses oneself. This is what I mean by insecurity. In fact, spirit-lessness can utter the same words the richest spirit has uttered, only it does not utter them by virtue of spirit. Man when he is characterized as spirit-less has become a talking-machine, and there is nothing to prevent him from learning a philosophical rigmarole just as easily as a confession of faith and a political recitative repeated by rote. Is it not remarkable that the only ironist and the greatest humorist[11] agreed with one another in saying what seems the simplest thing of all, that one must distinguish between what one understands and what one does not understand? And what is there to prevent the most spirit-less man from saying this same thing verbatim? There is only one attestation of spirit, and that is the attestation of the spirit within oneself. Anyone who requires another proof may perhaps stumble upon proofs in superabundance, but nevertheless he is already classified as spirit-less.

In spirit-lessness there is no dread. It is too happy and content for that, and too spirit-less. But this is a pitiful reason, and in this respect paganism differs from spirit-lessness for the fact that it is oriented in the direction *towards* spirit, the other in the direction *away from* it. Paganism therefore, if you please, is absence of spirit, and as such it is very different from spirit-lessness. To that extent paganism is much to be preferred. Spirit-lessness is stagnation of the spirit and the caricature of ideality. Hence spirit-lessness is not, properly speaking, dumb when it is a question of rigmarole, but it is *dumb* in the sense of which it is said of salt, "When salt becomes dumb,[12] wherewith can it be salted?" Precisely in this consists its perdition, but also its sense of security, namely, that it understands nothing spiritually, takes hold of nothing as a task, even if it is able to fumble at everything with its feeble clamminess. If on a particular occasion it is moved by spirit, and commences for an instant to kick like the galvanized leg of a frog, we have there a phenomenon which corresponds exactly to pagan fetishism. Spirit-lessness knows no authority, for it knows that over spirit there is no authority, but since unfortunately it is itself not spirit, it is in spite of its knowledge a complete idolater. It worships a dunce and a hero with the same adoration, but above all a charlatan is its real fetish.

Even though in spirit-lessness there is no dread, because this is excluded just as spirit is, yet dread is there, nevertheless, only it is waiting. One can imagine that a debtor has the luck to slip away from his creditor, to hold him off with mere talk; but one creditor there is who never had the worst of it, and that is the spirit. Viewed from the standpoint of the spirit, dread is present also in spirit-lessness, but hidden and masked. Even the onlooker shudders at the sight of it; for as the figure of dread, if one would let the imagination portray such a thing, is terrible to behold, its figure would terrify still more at such time as it finds it necessary to disguise itself in order not to appear to be what it is, although it is that all the same. When death appears in its true form as the lean and joyless reaper, one does not behold it without terror; but when, to mock men who imagine they can mock it, it comes upon the scene disguised, when only the spectator sees that this is death, this unknown figure which captivates all by his courtesy and causes all to exult in the wild abandonment of pleasure—then a profound horror seizes him.

§2

Dread dialectically determined in view of fate

GENERALLY we are accustomed to say that paganism lies in sin, perhaps it might be better to say that it lies in dread. Paganism upon the whole is sensuousness, but this is a sensuousness which has a relation to spirit, although the spirit in the deepest sense is not yet posited as spirit. But precisely this possibility is dread.

If then we ask further what is the object of dread, the answer as usual must be that it is nothing. Dread and nothing regularly correspond to one another. So soon as the actuality of freedom and of the spirit is posited, dread is annulled (*aufgehoben*). But what then is signified more particularly by the nothing of dread? It is fate.

Fate is a relation to spirit as something external, it is a relation between a spirit and another which is not spirit, and with which nevertheless it has to stand in a spiritual relationship. Fate may mean two things exactly opposite, since it is a unity of necessity and chance. This has not always been pointed out. Much has been said about the pagan *fatum* (this being in turn variously modified in the Oriental and in the Greek interpretation) as if it were necessity. A vestige of this necessity has been suffered to remain in the Christian view, where it came to mean fate, i.e. the accidental which cannot be made commensurable with providence. That, however, is not the true sense, for fate is precisely the unity of necessity and chance. This is ingeniously expressed by representing fate as blind, for that which walks forward blindly walks just as much by necessity as by chance. A necessity which is not conscious of itself is *eo ipso*, in relation to the next instant, chance. Fate then is the nothing of dread. It is nothing, for so soon as the spirit is posited dread is annulled; but fate is too, for thereby providence also is posited. One can say therefore of fate as Paul says of an idol, that "it is nothing in the world"—but the idol nevertheless is the object of the pagan's religiousness.

So in fate the dread of the pagan has its object, its nothing. The pagan cannot come into relation with fate, for one instant it is necessity, the next instant it is chance. And yet he *is* in relation to it, and this relation is dread. Nearer to fate than this the pagan cannot come. The attempt paganism made was penetrating enough to cast a new light upon it. He who has to explain fate must be just as ambiguous as fate is. And this too the *oracle* was. But in turn the oracle might mean exactly the opposite. So the relation of the pagan to the oracle is again dread. In this fact lies the profound and inexplicable tragic of paganism. The tragic, however, does not lie in the fact that the utterance of the oracle is ambiguous, but in the fact that the pagan could not forbear to take counsel of it. He is in relation to it and dare not refrain from consulting it. Even at the moment of taking counsel he is in an ambiguous relation to it (sympathetic and antipathetic). And think then of the explanations given by the oracle!

The concept of guilt and sin does not in the deepest sense emerge in paganism. If it had emerged, paganism would have foundered upon the contradiction that one might become guilty by fate. This indeed is the supreme contradiction, and in this contradiction Christianity breaks forth. Paganism does not comprehend it; for that it is too frivolous in its definition of the concept of guilt.

The concept of guilt and sin posits precisely the single individual as the single individual. There is no question of any relation to the whole world or to anything that is past. It is a question only of a man being guilty, and yet he must become guilty by fate, by that therefore of which there was no question, and thereby he must become that which precisely annuls the concept of fate, and this he must become by fate.

This contradiction, interpreted in a mistaken way, gives the mistaken concept of original sin; rightly understood, it gives the correct concept, namely, that every individual is himself and the race, and that the later individual is not essentially different from the first. In the possibility of dread freedom succumbs, overwhelmed by fate. Then its actuality rises up, but with the explanation that it became guilty. Dread at the extremest point where it seems as if the individual had become guilty is not yet guilt. So sin comes neither as a necessity nor by chance, and therefore to the concept of sin corresponds providence.

Within Christianity the dread in relation to fate which is characteristic of paganism is found wherever spirit, though it is present, is not essentially posited as spirit. This phenomenon reveals itself clearly when one observes a genius. Genius is immediacy as such, with the subjectivity preponderating.[13] Not yet is it posited as spirit, for as such it is posited only by spirit. As "immediate" it can be spirit (in this consists the deceptive appearance which suggests that the extraordinary gifts are spirit posited by spirit) but has then another outside of it which is not spirit, and is itself in an external relation to spirit. Therefore the genius is constantly discovering fate, and the deeper the genius, the deeper he discovers it. To spirit-lessness this of course is foolishness, but in reality it is grandeur; for no man is born with the idea of providence, and they who think that one acquires it gradually by education are greatly in error, though by this I do not mean to deny the importance of education. Genius displays its primitive might precisely in the discovery of fate, and thereby in turn displays its impotence. To the immediate spirit, which genius always is (only that it is an immediate spirit *sensu eminentiori*), fate is a limit. Providence is first posited in sin. Therefore the genius has a prodigious struggle to reach it. If he does not reach it, one can find in him a good subject for the study of fate.

Genius is an omnipotent "in-itself" (*Ansich*)[14] which as such would rock the world; therefore to preserve order another power comes into being along with it, and that is fate. Fate is nothing; it is the genius himself who discovers it, and the deeper his genius is, the more deeply he discovers it; for that figure is merely the anticipation of providence. If he continues to be merely a genius and does not turn back upon himself inwardly, he will accomplish astounding things, and yet he will constantly succumb before fate, if not outwardly and in a way which is tangible and visible to all, at least inwardly. Therefore the existence of a genius is always like a tale of romantic adventure, if in the deepest sense he does not succeed in turning back into himself. The genius is able to do all things and yet is dependent upon an insignificance which nobody comprehends, an insignificance upon which the genius himself by his almighty power bestows an almighty significance. Hence a second lieutenant, if he is a genius, is able to become an emperor, to remodel the world, so that there remains only one empire and one emperor. But hence also the army may be drawn up for battle, the absolutely favorable condition may the next instant perhaps be lost, a nation of heroes may implore that the order to attack be given, but he cannot, he must wait until the fourteenth of June. And why? Because that was the date of the Battle of Marengo. Hence everything may be in readiness, he himself standing in front of the legions, waiting only for the sun to rise as a signal for the speech which is to electrify the soldiers, and the sun may rise with a splendor greater than ever, a spectacle which exalts and enflames the army—but not him, for with such splendor it did not rise at Austerlitz, and only the sun of Austerlitz gives victory and enthusiasm. Hence the inexplicable passion with which such a man can rave against a perfectly insignificant person, although usually he is able to show humanity and amiability even towards his enemies. Yea, woe to the man, woe to the woman, woe to the innocent child, woe to the beast of the field, woe to the bird whose flight, woe to the tree whose branch comes in his way at the moment when he is to take his omen.

The external fact as such means nothing to the genius, therefore no one can understand him. It all depends upon how he himself understands it in the presence of his secret friend (fate). All may be lost, the simplest man and the shrewdest may unite in dissuading him from the fruitless endeavor. The genius, however, knows that he is stronger than the whole world, provided at this point no doubtful commentary is found of the invisible writing in which he reads the will of fate. If he reads it according to his wish, then with his omnipotent voice he says to the captain of the boat, "Sail on, you are carrying Caesar and his fortune."[15] All may be won, and that same instant he receives the report, perhaps there is in it a word the significance of which no creature, not God in heaven, understands (for in a certain sense not even God understands the genius)—and with that he collapses impotently.

Genius is thus outside the general. It is great by reason of its belief in fate, whether it conquers or falls, for it conquers by itself and falls by itself, or rather both come about by fate. Commonly the man of genius is admired for his greatness only when he conquers, yet he is never greater than when he falls by his own act. This must be understood to apply to the case where fate does not declare itself in an external way. In this case, where precisely at the instant when, humanly speaking, all is won, the genius discovers the doubtful reading in the text and then collapses, one may well exclaim, "What a giant it would take to overthrow him!" Therefore no one could do it, except himself. The faith which subdues kingdoms and lands under his mighty hand, while men believed it was a fairy tale, this same faith overthrew him, and his fall was a still more unfathomable tale.

Hence the genius is in dread at a different point of time than men generally are. They discover danger only at the instant of danger, till then they feel secure, and when the danger is past they again feel secure. The genius is strongest in the instant of danger; on the other hand, his dread lies in the instant before and the instant after, this trembling moment when he must hold converse with that great unknown which is fate. Perhaps his dread is greatest precisely the instant after, because the impatience of certitude always increases in inverse ratio to the distance, since there is constantly more and more to lose the nearer one has come to victory, and most of all at the instant of victory, and because the consistency of fate is precisely inconsistency.

Genius as such cannot comprehend itself religiously, therefore it does not get so far as sin and providence, and for this reason it is a relation of dread to fate. Never has there existed any genius without this dread, unless at the same time it has been religious.

If genius remains immediately determined and turns outward, it becomes indeed great, and its exploits astounding, but it never comes to itself, and it never becomes great in its own eyes. All its activity is outwardly directed, but, if I may so speak, the planetarian nucleus from which everything radiates does not come into existence. The significance of genius for itself is null, or it is just as obviously melancholy as is the sympathy with which the inhabitants of the Faroe Islands would rejoice, if on one of these islands there lived a native Faroese who by his works in various European languages astonished all Europe, who transformed the sciences by his immortal contributions, but on the other hand never wrote a line in the language of the Faroes, and at last forgot how to speak it. To itself genius does not in the deepest sense become significant, its compass can extend no higher than the determinants of fate in relation to good luck, bad luck, glory, honor, power, undying fame, all of which are temporal determinants. Every deeper dialectical determinant of dread is excluded. The utmost would be that the genius might be regarded as guilty, in such a way that dread is not directed towards guilt but towards the appearance of it, which is a determinant of honor. This psychic state would be an appropriate one for poetic treatment. Such a condition may be the lot of any man, but the genius would grasp it so profoundly that he would not be striving with men but with the profoundest mysteries of existence.

That in spite of its luster and glory and significance the existence of such a genius is sin, is a truth which requires courage to understand, and one will hardly understand it before one has learned to satisfy the hunger of the wishful soul. Nevertheless it is true. Nothing is proved by the consideration that such an existence may after all be happy. One may in fact conceive of one's gifts as a means of diversion, and in realizing that effect may at no instant raise oneself above the determinants of which the temporal consists. Only through a religious reflection are genius and talent justified in the deepest sense. If one will take for example a genius like Talleyrand, it is evident that in him there was the possibility of a far deeper reflection upon life. This he avoided. He followed the determinant in him which turned outward. His much admired genius for intrigue was gloriously demonstrated. His elasticity, the saturation point of his genius (to employ a term the chemists use with reference to corrosive acids) is admired, but he belongs to the temporal. If such a genius had disdained the temporal as the immediate, had turned towards himself and towards the divine, what a religious genius might have come out of it! But also what torments he would have had to experience! It is an alleviation in life to follow the immediate determinants, whether one be great or small, but the reward also is in proportion to the effort, whether one be great or small, and the man who is not so spiritually ripe as to comprehend that even immortal honor throughout all generations is after all only a determinant of the temporal, as to comprehend that the aspiration after this which keeps men's souls sleepless with wish and desire is something very imperfect in comparison with the immortality which is for every man and which would rightly arouse the justifiable envy of all the world, if it were reserved for only one man—he will not get far in his explanation of spirit and immortality.

§3

Dread dialectically defined
in view of guilt

It is commonly said that Judaism represents the standpoint of the law. This, however, may be expressed also by saying that Judaism lies in dread. But here the nothing of dread denotes something else than fate. It is in this sphere that the formula "dread—nothing" appears most paradoxical, for after all guilt is something. It is correct, nevertheless, and so long as guilt is the object of dread it is nothing. The ambiguity lies in the relation; for so soon as guilt is posited, dread is gone, and repentance is there. The relation, as it always is with dread, is sympathetic and antipathetic. This again seems paradoxical, and yet it is not; for though dread is afraid, yet it maintains a sly intercourse with its object, cannot look away from it, indeed will not, for if the individual wills this, then repentance sets in. If to one or another this may appear a difficult saying, I can do nothing about it. He who has the requisite firmness to be, if I may use the expression, a prosecuting attorney for the Deity, though not with respect to others, yet with respect to himself, will not find this saying difficult. Life moreover presents phenomena enough in which the individual in dread gazes almost desirously at guilt and yet fears it. Guilt, like the eye of the serpent, has the power to fascinate spirit.

At this point lies the truth in the Carpocratian[16] notion of attaining perfection through sin. It has truth at the instant of decision when the immediate spirit is positing itself as spirit by spirit. On the other hand, it is a blasphemy to think that the principle should be carried out *in concreto*.

Precisely by this fact [its dread of guilt] Judaism is further advanced than Hellenism, and in this one can perceive the sympathetic factor in the relation of dread to guilt, which Judaism would not relinquish at any price for the sake of acquiring the lighter expressions of Hellenism: fate, luck, misfortune.

Dread in Judaism is dread of guilt. Guilt is a power which spreads abroad everywhere, and which yet no one in a deeper sense can understand, though it broods over existence. That which is to explain it must therefore partake of the same character [of not being understood], just as the oracle corresponded to fate. To the oracle of paganism corresponds the sacrifice of Judaism. But for this reason neither can the sacrifice be understood by anyone. Therein consists the profound tragedy of Judaism, analogous to the pagan's relation to the oracle. The Jew has recourse to the sacrifice, but that is of no help to him, for what properly must help him would be that the relation of dread to guilt was annulled [*aufgehoben*] and a real relation posited. Inasmuch as this does not come to pass, the sacrifice becomes ambiguous, a fact which is expressed by its repetition, a further consequence of which would be a pure scepticism with respect to the act of sacrifice itself.

What resulted in the foregoing discussion, that only with sin is providence posited, recurs here in the form that only with sin is atonement posited; and its sacrifice is not repeated. This is not due to the outward perfection of the sacrifice, if I may so speak, but the perfection of the sacrifice corresponds to the actual situation of sin as posited. So long as the actual situation of sin is not posited, the sacrifice must be repeated. (Thus the sacrifice was in fact repeated in Catholicism, although the absolute perfection of the sacrifice is recognized.)

What has been briefly indicated here with reference to universal history is repeated within Christianity in the individualities. Here again genius evinces clearly what in less original men exists in such a way that it cannot easily be reduced to categories. By and large the genius differs from other men merely in the fact that within his historical presuppositions he consciously begins just as originally as Adam did. Every time a genius is born, existence as it were is put to the test; for he surveys and lives through all the past until he catches up with himself. The knowledge the genius has of the past is therefore entirely different from that which is offered by outlines of universal history.

That the genius may remain in his immediateness was indicated in the foregoing discussion, and the explanation that this is sin implies at the same time genuine courtesy towards genius. Every human life is planned religiously. To wish to deny this is to throw everything into confusion and to annul the concepts of individual, race, immortality. It is to be wished that men would bring their perspicacity to bear upon this point, for here lie very difficult problems. To say of a man who has an intriguing mind that he should be a diplomat or a detective, of one who has mimic talents for comedy that he should be an actor, of a man who has no talent at all that he should be a stoker in the Court House, is to have a very fatuous view of life, or rather to have no view at all, for all this is a matter of course. But to explain how my religious existence comes into relation with and expresses itself in my outward situation, that is the problem. But in our time who troubles himself to think of such things?—in spite of the fact that now more than ever this present life appears to be a fleeting and transitory instant. But instead of learning to grasp the eternal, one learns only to kill [chase life out of] oneself and one's neighbor with fatigue by chasing the instant. If only one can join the party, if merely on a single occasion one can lead the dance of the instant, then one has lived, then one has become the envy of the unfortunates who, though they were not born but tumbled head over heels into the world and go on tumbling, never attain this. Then one has lived! For what more is a human life worth than the brief loveliness of a young girl who has lasted uncommonly well if for one night she has enchanted the line of dancers and faded only at dawn? To consider how a religious existence penetrates and saturates the outward situation, one has no time. Even if one is not chasing with the haste of despair, one grasps only what lies nearest. In that way one becomes perhaps something great in the world. If, besides, one goes once in a while to church, then everything is superlatively good. This seems to indicate that for some individuals religion is the absolute, for others not,* and then good-night to all meaning in life. The deliberation becomes of course more difficult the more remote the task is from the religious as such. What profound religious reflection it would require to approach such an external task, for example, as that of being a comic actor! That this can be done I do not deny, for he who has some understanding of the religious knows that it is more ductile than gold and absolutely commensurable. The fault of the Middle Ages[17] was not the religious reflection but that men came to a stop too soon. Here reappears the question of repetition, that is to say, the question in what measure an individual after having begun the religious reflection can get himself back again whole from head to heel. In the Middle Ages they broke off abruptly. So, at the moment when the individual had to take himself back again, he stumbled, for example over the fact that he possessed wit, a sense for the comic, etc., then promptly annihilated all this as something very imperfect. Nowadays one discovers only too easily that such a thing is foolishness, for if a man has wit and a talent for comedy, he is a Pamphilius of good fortune—and what more can a man want? Such explanations have of course not the remotest presentiment of the problem, for though men in our times are born more worldly-wise than in the old days, they are also many of them born blind so far as religion is concerned. Yet in the Middle Ages here are cases to be found in which the deliberation was carried turther. For example, when a painter interpreted his talent religiously, but this talent could not express itself in the productions which lie closest to the religious sphere, one has seen in this situation that such an artist could just as piously devote himself to painting a Venus, just as piously interpret his artistic calling as did he who helped the Church by enthralling the eyes of the congregation with the sight of heavenly beauty. However, in view of all such cases, we have yet to wait until there come forward individuals who, in spite of their outward gifts, do not choose the

* Among the Greeks the question about the religious could not emerge in this form. Yet it is very pretty to read what Plato somewhere recounts and applies.[18] When Epimetheus had furnished men with all sorts of gifts, he asked Zeus whether he should now distribute the capacity to choose between good and evil the same way he had distributed the other gifts, so that one might get this capacity just as another got the gift of eloquence, another the gift of poetry, another the gift of art. But Zeus replied that this capacity should be distributed as a whole to all, because to every man alike it belonged essentially.

broad way, but rather pain and distress and dread, upon which religious minds reflect and reflect for so long a time that they lose as it were what it is only too seductive and dangerous to possess. Such a battle is indubitably very exhausting, since there will come moments when they almost regret having started upon this path, and sadly, yea, sometimes almost despairingly, they will think of the smiling path which would have stretched before them if they had followed the immediate bent of talent. Yet indubitably, in the extremest dismay of distress, when it is as though all were lost, because the path along which he would advance is impassable and the smiling path of talent is barred by his own act, the man who is attentive will hear a voice which says, "Well, my son, go forward nevertheless, for he who loses all gains all."

We will now consider the religious genius, that is, a genius who is not willing to stop with his immediateness. Whether he will ever get to the point of turning outwards, remains for him a subsequent question. The first thing he does is to turn towards himself. As the immediate genius had fate, so he has guilt as the figure which follows him. For by the fact that he turns towards himself he turns *eo ipso* towards God, and it is a well-established ceremonial convention that if the finite spirit would see God it must begin by being guilty. In turning towards himself he discovers guilt. The greater the genius, the more profoundly he discovers guilt. That to the spirit-less this is foolishness, is to me a joy and a glad token. The genius is not "as people mostly are," and he is not content with that. This is not due to disdain of men, but it is because he is primitively concerned with himself, while all other men and their explanations are no help to him.

The fact that he discovers guilt so profoundly shows that to him this concept is present *sensu eminentiori*, as is also its opposite, innocence. So it was with the immediate genius in relation to fate; for every man has some little relation to fate, but there it ends... in twaddle, which does not notice what Talleyrand (and Young[19] before him) discovered, and yet did not express so perfectly as twaddle does, that language exists in order to conceal thoughts— that is, to conceal the fact that one has none.

So by turning inwardly he discovers freedom. Fate he does not fear, for he lays hold of no external task, and for him freedom is his bliss, not freedom to do this or that in the world, to become king and emperor, or the exponent of popular opinion, but freedom to know of himself that he is freedom. Yet the higher an individual rises, the dearer the price he must pay for everything, and as a precautionary measure there comes into being along with this *Ansich* of freedom another figure, guilt. This, like fate to the pagan, is the only thing he fears, but his fear is not the fear of being thought guilty, as in the foregoing case it was as a maximum, but fear of being guilty. In the degree that he discovers freedom, in that same degree does the dread of guilt in the condition of possibility impend over him. Guilt only does he fear, for that is the one and only thing that can deprive him of freedom. It is easily seen that freedom is not defiance by any means, or the selfish liberty understood in a finite sense. By such an assumption [that of *liberum arbitrium*] the effort has often been made to explain the origin of sin. That, however, is labor lost, for the assumption of such a presupposition presents a greater difficulty than that which it would explain. When freedom is so interpreted, its opposite is necessity, which shows that freedom has been construed under an intellectual category. No, the opposite of freedom is guilt, and it is the supreme glory of freedom that it has only with itself to do, that it projects guilt in its possibility and also posits it by itself, and if guilt is posited actually, freedom still posits it by itself. If one does not give heed to this, then one has confounded freedom with something entirely different, with *force*.

When freedom then fears guilt, it is not that it fears to recognize itself as guilty, if it is guilty, but it fears to become guilty, and therefore, so soon as guilt is posited, freedom comes back again as repentance. But meanwhile freedom's relation to guilt is a possibility. Here genius shows itself again by not leaping away from the primitive decision, by not seeking the decision outside itself with Tom, Dick and Harry, by not being content with the usual haggling. Only by itself can freedom learn to know whether it is freedom or guilt which is posited. There is nothing therefore more ludicrous than to assume that the question whether one is a sinner and guilty belongs under the rubric: lesson to be learned verbatim.

The relation of freedom to guilt is dread, because freedom and guilt are still a possibility. But when freedom is thus with all its wishful passion staring at itself, and would keep guilt at a distance so that not a jot of it might be found in freedom, it is not able to refrain from staring at guilt, and this staring is the ambiguity of dread, just as the very act of renunciation within possibility is a yearning.

Here then is the place where it appears clearly enough in what sense there is a "more" in the dread of the later individual in comparison with the dread of Adam.* Guilt in this case is a more concrete notion, which in the relation of possibility to freedom becomes more and more possible. At last it is as if the guilt of the whole world united to make him guilty, or in other words, as if by becoming guilty he became guilty of the guilt of the whole world. Guilt has, it is true, the dialectical characteristic that it is not transferable, but he who becomes guilty becomes guilty of that "by and with" which guilt was occasioned, for guilt never has an external occasion, and he who falls into temptation is himself guilty of the temptation.

In the situation of possibility this [dread] manifests itself in the form of illusion, but so soon as repentance breaks forth with the actual sin, dread has the actual sin as its object. With respect to the possibility of freedom it holds good that the more profoundly guilt is discovered, the greater is the genius; for man's greatness depends solely upon the energy of the God-relationship in him, even though this God-relationship finds an altogether erroneous expression as fate.

So then just as fate at last catches the immediate genius, and this is in reality his culminating instant, not therefore the glittering outward realization which amazes men and even calls artisans from their daily occupations to gape, but the instant when by himself he collapses before himself by fate; so does guilt catch the religious genius, and this is the instant of culmination, the instant when he is strongest, not the instant when the sight of his piety is like the festivity of a solemn day of rest, but when by himself he sinks before himself into the abyss of the consciousness of sin.

* However, one must not forget that here the analogy is inexact, inasmuch as in the case of the later individual it is not with innocence we have to do, but with the repressed consciousness of sin.

CHAPTER IV

The Dread in Sin, or
Dread as the Consequence of Sin in the
Particular Individual

B
Y THE qualitative leap sin came into the world, and in this
way it is continually coming into it. One might think that
so soon as sin is posited dread would be annulled, dread
having been defined as freedom's appearance before itself in possibility. The qualitative leap is indeed reality, and by this, as it
seems, possibility must be annulled, and dread, too. However,
such is not the case. In the first place, reality is not just one single
factor; in the second place, the reality here posited is an illegitimate
reality. So dread comes back again in relation to what was posited
and in relation to the future. Now, however, dread has a definite
object, its nothing is now really something, since the difference
between good and evil* is posited *in concreto*, and dread therefore

* The problem, What is the good? is a problem which comes closer and closer
to our age, because it is of decisive importance for the question about the relation between Church and State and morals. In making answer to that question
one must be cautious. Hitherto "the true" has, strangely enough, enjoyed a
position of pre-eminence, owing to the fact that the trilogy: the true, the beautiful, the good, was interpreted and presented...in the true, i.e. the understanding.
The good cannot be defined. The good is freedom. The first distinction between
good and evil is for and in freedom, and this distinction is never *in abstracto*
but always *in concreto*. Hence for one who is not thoroughly conversant with
the Socratic method it proves disturbing that by Socrates the good, this apparently infinite abstraction, is instantly applied to the most concrete cases. The
method is perfectly correct, except that he did amiss (to the Greek way of
thinking he did rightly) in conceiving the good from its outward side (the
useful, the finitely teleological). The distinction between good and evil certainly
exists for freedom, but not *in abstracto*. The misunderstanding at this point is
due to the fact that freedom is commonly conceived as something other than
it is, namely, as an object of thought. But freedom is never *in abstracto*. If one
would grant freedom an instant to make a choice between good and evil, without
being itself in either of the two positions, then precisely at that instant freedom
is not freedom but a meaningless reflection. And to what end does this experiment serve except to confuse? In case (*sit venia verbo*) freedom remains in the
good, it knows nothing at all of the evil. In this sense one may say of God
(if anyone would misunderstand me, it is not my fault) that He knows nothing
of evil. By this I do not mean to say that the evil is the negative, *das Aufzu-
hebende* [what has to be annulled]; but the fact that God does not know of it,
cannot and will not know of it, is the absolute punishment of the evil. In this
sense the preposition ἀπό is used in the New Testament to indicate remoteness

has lost its dialectical ambiguity. This applies to Adam as it does to every later individual, for with respect to the qualitative leap they are completely alike.

When sin is posited in the particular individual by the qualitative leap, the distinction is then posited between good and evil. We have nowhere been chargeable with the foolishness of thinking that man *must* sin; on the contrary, we have everywhere protested against every sort of merely experimental knowledge, and have said, what we here again repeat, that sin presupposes itself, just as freedom does, and cannot be explained, any more than freedom can, by any antecedent. To let freedom commence as a *liberum arbitrium* (which nowhere is to be found, as Leibnitz says[1]), which is quite as free to choose the good as the evil, is to make every explanation radically impossible. To talk about good and evil as the objects of freedom is to finitize both freedom and the concepts of good and evil. Freedom is infinite and does not arise out of anything. Therefore to want to say that man sins necessarily is to want to construe the curve of the leap as a straight line. That such a procedure appears to many very plausible is due to the fact that lack of thought seems to many men the most natural thing in the world, and that at all times the number of those men is legion who regard as praiseworthy a way of thinking which throughout the centuries has in vain been branded as λόγος ἀργός (Chrysippus), *ignava ratio* (Cicero), *sophisma pigrum, la raison paresseuse* (Leibnitz).[2]

Now again psychology has dread as the object of its study, but it must be cautious. The history of the individual life goes forward in a movement from state to state. Every state is posited by a leap. In this way sin came into the world, and so does it continue to come, unless it is stopped. Yet every repetition of it is not a simple consequence but a new leap. Every such leap is preceded by a state, which is the closest approximation to the leap psychology can attain. This state is the object of psychological study. In every state there is a possibility present, and to that extent there is a

from God, God's ignoring of evil, if I dare say so. When God is conceived finitely, it is convenient enough for the evil to have God ignore it; but since God is the infinite, His ignoring it is the most vivid expression of annihilation; for the evil cannot dispense with God, even if it were merely in order to be the evil. I will quote a passage from Scripture. In 2 Thessalonians 1:9 it is said of them that know not God and obey not the Gospel: οἵτινες δίκην τίσουσιν ὄλεθρον αἰώνιον ἀπὸ προσώπου τοῦ κυρίου καὶ ἀπὸ τῆς δόξης τῆς ἰσκύος αὐτοῦ.

dread. Such is the case after sin is posited, for only in the good is there a unity of the given situation, and transition.

§ 1

Dread of the evil

(a). The posited sin is, to be sure, a possibility annulled (*aufgehoben*), but at the same time it is an unwarranted reality. That being the case, dread can be related to it. Since it is an unwarranted reality, it ought in turn to be negated. This labor remorse is ready to undertake. Here is the field for the cunning sophistry of dread. While the reality of sin holds one hand of freedom in its icy grasp, as the Commandant held Don Juan,[3] with the other hand it gesticulates with illusion, deceit, and the eloquence of hallucination.*

(b). The posited sin is at the same time in itself a consequence, even though it is a consequence foreign to freedom. This consequence announces itself, and dread is related to the future of this consequence, which is the possibility of a new state. However deep the individual has sunk, he may sink still deeper, and this "may" is the object of dread. The more relaxed dread becomes, the more clearly it indicates that the consequence of sin has filled the individual in *succum et sanguinem*, and that sin has acquired the right of naturalization in the individuality.

Sin here of course means the concrete, for one never sins generally or abstractly. Even the sin† of wishing to return and find oneself back before the reality of sin is not a sin in general, and indeed such an abstract sin has never been met with. He who has some knowledge of men knows very well that sophistry has a way of perpetually picking up a particular point and perpetually varying it. Dread would have the reality of sin removed, but only to a certain degree; or rather it would have the reality continue, but, *nota bene*, only to a certain degree. Therefore it even is not disinclined to flirt with quantitative determinants. Indeed, the more developed dread is, the further it ventures to carry this flirtation;

---

* In view of the form of this investigation I can indicate the particular situations only very briefly, almost algebraically. There is no room here for a thorough description of them.

† This is said from the point of view of ethics; for ethics does not see the state, but it sees how the state is at the same instant a new sin.

but so soon as the jest and diversion of the quantitative determinants is about to catch the individual in the qualitative leap, which lies in wait like the ant-lion in the funnel of loose sand, dread cautiously retires, then it has a little point which must be saved and which is without sin, and the next instant another point. A consciousness of sin profoundly and seriously carried out in the expression of remorse is a great rarity. Nevertheless, I shall take care for my own sake, for the sake of sound thinking, and for the neighbor's sake, not to express the situation as Schelling[4] presumably would, who somewhere speaks of "genius for work" in the same sense as he would speak of genius for music, etc. Thus it is that sometimes, without being aware of it, a person may by the use of one illustrative word bring everything to naught. If every man does not essentially participate in the absolute, then the whole game's up. In the sphere of religion, therefore, one should not talk of genius as a special gift, for here the "gift" is simply to will, and the man who does not will we ought to hold at least in sufficient respect not to pity him [for his lack of gifts].

Ethically speaking, sin is not a state or condition. The state, however, is the closest psychological approximation to the next state. Dread is now constantly present as the possibility of the new state. In the state first described, under (a), dread is more observable, whereas in (b) it disappears more and more. But nevertheless it is lurking outside such an individual, and seen from the standpoint of spirit it is then greater than at any time. In (a) it is dread in view of the reality of sin, out of which sophistry produces possibility, whereas ethically viewed it sins in doing so. Here the movement of dread is the opposite of that in the state of innocence, where out of the possibility of sin, psychologically speaking, it produces reality, whereas ethically viewed this comes with the qualitative leap. In (b) it is dread in view of the future possibility of sin. If at this point dread decreases, we explain this by the fact that the consequence of sin triumphs.

(c). The posited sin is an unwarranted reality; it is reality, and by the individual it is posited as reality in remorse, but remorse does not become the freedom of the individual. Remorse is reduced to a possibility in relation to sin; in other words, remorse cannot annul sin, it can only sorrow over it. Sin goes forward in its consequence, remorse follows it step by step, but always an instant too late. It compels itself to look at the horror, but it is like mad

King Lear ("O thou ruined masterpiece of nature!"⁵). It has lost the reins of government and has strength left only to repine. Here dread is at its highest pitch. Remorse has lost its senses, and dread is potentiated to remorse. The consequence of sin goes on, it drags the individual with it as a woman is dragged by the hangman with his hand in her hair, while she shrieks in desperation. Remorse is in advance, it discovers the consequence before it comes, as we may have a presentiment of an approaching storm; the consequence comes nearer, the individual trembles, like a horse which balks and neighs at the spot where once it took fright. Sin conquers. Dread throws itself despairingly into the arms of remorse. Remorse ventures its utmost. It interprets the consequence of sin as penal suffering, and perdition as a consequence of sin. It is lost, its doom is pronounced, its condemnation is certain, and the aggravation of the sentence is that the individual shall throughout his life be dragged to the place of execution. In other words, remorse has become insane.

What here is indicated, life may furnish occasions to observe. Such a state is rarely found among natures wholly depraved, but generally only among the deeper sort of men; for it requires a great deal of primitiveness and persistence in the mad energy of will not to come under the categories (a) or (b). The sophistry which insane remorse is every instant capable of producing, no dialectic is able to overcome. Such a remorse has a contrition which is more powerful in its dialectic and in its expression of passion than the true remorse. In another sense, of course, it is more impotent; yet it is remarkable, as anyone who has observed such cases has certainly remarked, what persuasiveness and what eloquence such a remorse possesses to disarm every objection, to convince all who come near it—only to despair of itself again when this diversion is over. To try to put a stop to this horror by words and phrases is labor lost, and he who dreams of doing such a thing may count upon it that his preachifying will be like infantile babble in comparison with the elemental eloquence which is at the service of such remorse. This phenomenon may show itself quite as well in relation to sensual vices (addiction to drink, to opium, to debauchery, etc.) as in relation to the higher vices (pride, vanity, wrath, hatred, defiance, craftiness, etc.). The individual may rue his wrath, and the more profound he is, the more profound is remorse. But remorse cannot make him free, in that expectation he is mistaken. The occasion comes, dread has already discovered it, every thought trembles, dread sucks like a vampire the strength of remorse and shakes its head; it is as though wrath had already conquered, dread already has a presentiment of freedom's contrition which is reserved for the next instant. The instant comes, wrath conquers.

Whatever the consequence of sin may be, the fact that the phenomenon is exhibited on a considerable scale is always an indication of a deeper nature. The fact that one sees it rather rarely in life, or in other words that one must be a trained observer in order to see it more frequently, is due to the fact that it is a phenomenon which can be concealed, and that also it is often suppressed by an abortion, men having several prudential devices for suppressing this embryo of the highest life. No more is needed than to take counsel with Tom, Dick, and Harry—with that one becomes at once what "people mostly are," and can always be assured of the testimony of several reliable men that one is all of that. The most efficacious means of liberation from the assaults of the spirit is to become spirit-less, the sooner the better. If only one takes care of that betimes, everything goes of itself, and as for the assaults of the spirit, one can explain that they simply do not exist, or regard them at the most as a piquant poetical fiction. The path to perfection was in old days narrow and lonesome, the pilgrimage disturbed by thoughts of despair, exposed to the robber assaults of sin, a target for the arrows of them that passed by, as dangerous as the shafts of the Scythian hordes—now one travels to perfection by railway,[6] in cheerful company, and before a word is heard of all this, one has arrived.

The one and only thing which is able to disarm the sophistry of remorse is faith, courage to believe that the state of sin is itself a new sin, courage to renounce dread without any dread, which only faith is capable of—not that it annihilates dread, but remaining ever young, it is continually developing itself out of the death throe of dread. Only faith is capable of doing this, for only in faith is the synthesis eternally and every instant possible.

It is not difficult to perceive that everything that has here been expounded belongs to the sphere of psychology. Ethically considered, everything depends upon getting the individual in the right position with regard to sin. So soon as he stands there, he stands remorseful in sin. The same instant, ideally regarded, he has recourse to dogmatics. Remorse is the utmost ethical contradiction, partly because ethics, requiring as it does ideality, must be content to accept remorse, partly because remorse remains dialectically ambiguous with regard to what it has to remove, which ambiguity dogmatics removes by the Atonement, in which the category of original sin becomes clear. Moreover, remorse delays action, and it is action that ethics specifically requires. At last remorse must become its own object, being remorseful for the fact that its movement becomes a deficit of action. It was therefore a genuine ethical outburst, full of energy and courage, when Fichte as an old man said that there was no time for remorse.[7] In saying this, however, he did not carry the word "remorse" to its dialectical apex, where in posing itself it will annul itself by a new remorse [repentance] and then collapse.

What has been expounded in this section, as indeed everywhere in this book, is what psychologically might be called the psychological attitudes which freedom assumes towards sin, or the psychological states approximating sin. It does not pretend to explain sin ethically.

§2

Dread of the good
(The demoniacal)

In our time there is seldom any question raised about the demoniacal. The particular examples of it found in the New Testament are commonly treated as doubtful. In so far as the theologians make an effort to explain them, they generally lose themselves in observations about this or another unnatural sin, in which they find also examples of the brutish nature gaining such an ascendancy over a man that it makes itself known by inarticulate animal sounds, or by mimicry of animal ways and a brutish look, whether it be that brutishness acquires in man a pronounced form (the physiognomic expression to which Lavater refers[8]), or in a flash like a disappearing express it suggests a presentiment of what dwells within, as the glance or gesture of a madman, in the space of an instant which is shorter than a blink of the eye, parodies, mocks, caricatures the sensible, discreet, intelligent man with whom one is talking. What the theologians say with regard to this may be quite true—but is it to the point? Generally the phenomenon is described in such a way that one sees clearly that it is a question of bondage to sin, a state which I cannot describe better than by recalling a game men play where two are concealed under a cloak, appearing to be one person, and while one speaks the other gesticulates without any pertinence to what is being said. For it is thus the beast has clothed itself in the form of the man and then caricatures him by gestures and byplay. But the bondage of sin is not yet the demoniacal. So soon as sin is posited and the individual remains in sin there are two formations, one of which we have described in the foregoing section. If one does not pay heed at this point, it will not be possible to define the demoniacal. The individual is in sin, and he is in dread of the evil. This formation, viewed from a higher standpoint, is in the good, and for this reason the individual is in dread of the evil. The other formation is the demoniacal. The individual is in the evil and is in dread of the good. The bondage of sin is an unfree relation to the evil, but the demoniacal is an unfree relation to the good.

The demoniacal becomes thoroughly evident only when it is touched by the good, which now comes to its confines from the outside. It is noteworthy therefore that in the New Testament the demoniacal shows itself only with Christ's coming in contact with it. Whether the demon is legion (cf. Matthew 8:28-34; Mark 5:1-20; Luke 8:26-39) or is dumb (cf. Luke 11:14) the phenomenon is the same, it is dread of the good; for dread can quite as well express itself by muteness as by loud cries. The good of course signifies to it the reintegration of freedom, redemption, salvation, or whatever name one would give it.

In earlier times there often was question about the demoniacal. It is of no importance here to make studies, or to have made studies,[9] which would enable one to patter or quote from learned and curious books. One can easily sketch the various views which are possible and at various times have also been actual. This may have some importance, since the diversity of the views may lead to a definition of the concept.

One can regard the demoniacal from the aesthetico-metaphysical point of view. The phenomenon then falls under the categories of misfortune, fate, etc., can be regarded as analogous with congenital lunacy, etc. One is then related to the phenomenon compassionately. But just as the wish is the most paltry solo art, so to be compassionate in this sense is the most paltry of all social virtuosities and dexterities. Compassion is so far from being an advantage to the sufferer that rather by it one is only protecting one's own egoism. One dare not in a deeper sense think of such troubles, and so one spares oneself by compassion. Only when the compassionate person is so related by his compassion to the sufferer that in the strictest sense he comprehends that it is his own cause which is here in question, only when he knows how to identify himself in such a way with the sufferer that when he is fighting for an explanation he is fighting for himself, renouncing all thoughtlessness, softness, and cowardice, only then does compassion acquire significance, and only then does it perhaps find a meaning, since the compassionate man differs from the sufferer for the fact that he suffers in a higher form. When compassion is related in this way to the demoniacal, it is not a question of the comforting word, or of the contribution of a mite, or of a shrug of the shoulder; for then if one groans, one has something to groan for. In case the demoniacal is fate, it can befall everyone. This is undeniable, even though in our cowardly age one does everything possible by way of diversions and the Janizary music of loud-voiced enterprises to keep lonely thoughts away, just as in the forests of America they keep away wild beasts by torches, by yells, by the sound of cymbals. Hence it is that in our age one learns to know so little about the highest spiritual temptations, but all the more about the coquettish conflicts between men, and between man and woman, which the refined life of society and the soirée brings in its train. If the genuine humane compassion assumes responsibility for suffering as surety and bondsman, it must first make clear to what extent it is fate and to what extent guilt. And this distinction must be drawn by the troubled but yet resolute passion of freedom, that one may dare to hold fast to it though the whole world were to come to ruin, even though it might seem that by one's own firmness one might cause irreparable harm.

The demoniacal has been ethically regarded with severe condemnation. It is well enough known with what terrible severity it has been pursued, discovered, punished. In our age one shudders at the accounts of this, one becomes sentimental, emotional, at the thought that in our age people do not act that way. This may quite well be so—but is this sentimental compassion so very much more commendable? It is not my part to judge or to condemn that conduct, but only to observe it. The fact that it was so ethically severe shows precisely that its compassion was of a better quality. By identifying itself in thought with the phenomenon it found no further explanation than that it was guilt. It was therefore convinced that after all in the last resort the demoniac himself, in accordance with his better possibility, must wish that every cruelty and severity might be employed against him.* Was it not—to take an example from a similar sphere—was it not Augustine who recommended punishment, yea, the punishment of death,[10] for heretics? Was it because he lacked compassion? Surely the difference between his conduct and that of our age was due rather to the fact that his compassion had not made him cowardly, so that with regard to himself he would have said, "If things were to come to such a pass with me, please God there might be a Church which would not abandon me but would employ all its force." But in our age people are afraid, as Socrates somewhere says,[11] of letting themselves be cut and cauterized for their healing.

The demoniacal has been regarded therapeutically. As a matter of course: *"Mit Pulver und mit Pillen"* [Take my powder and my pills]—and then clysters! Then the apothecary and the doctor put their heads together. The patient has been isolated so that the others might not be afraid. In our courageous age one does not say to a patient that he will die, one does not dare to call the priest for fear the patient may die of fright, one does not dare to say to the patient that the same day a man died of the same illness. The patient was isolated, compassion made inquiries about him, the physician promised to issue as soon as possible a tabulated statistical statement in order to determine the average. And when one has the average, everything is explained. The therapeutic way of viewing the case regards the phenomenon as purely physical and somatic, and it does as physicians often do, especially in Hoffmann's novels—it takes its pinch of snuff and says, "This is a serious case."

---

* The man who is not so ethically developed that he would find comfort and assuagement if, even when he was suffering most, one had the courage to say to him, "This is not fate, it is guilt," would not find comfort and assuagement when this was said to him honestly and earnestly, then that man is not in a great sense ethically developed; for the ethical individual fears nothing so much as fate and aesthetic folderol which under the cloak of compassion would trick him out of his treasure, viz. freedom.

The fact that such various ways of regarding it are possible shows how ambiguous is this phenomenon, and that in a way it belongs to all spheres, the somatic, the psychic, the pneumatic. This indicates that the demoniacal covers a far greater field than is commonly supposed, and this can be explained by the fact that man is a synthesis of soul and body supported by spirit, wherefore a disorganization in one shows itself in the others. But so soon as it is observed how large a field it covers, it will perhaps appear that even divers of those men who want to deal with this phenomenon come themselves under the same category, and that a trace of this is to be found in every man, as sure as every man is a sinner.

But since the demoniacal has in the course of time denoted all sorts of things, and has at last been promoted to mean anything you please, it would be well to define the concept a little. It must be noted that already we have assigned it to its proper place. In innocence there can be no question of the demoniacal. On the other hand, we must give up every fantastic notion of a pact with the devil, etc., whereby a man became absolutely evil. To this was due the contradiction in the behavior of the earlier time. People assumed this fantastic notion, and yet they would punish. Yet the punishment itself was not merely self-defense but was inflicted in order that at the same time the persons concerned might be saved, either by a milder punishment or by the penalty of death. But if there could be any question of salvation, the individual was after all not entirely in the power of evil; and if he were entirely in the power of evil, it would be a contradiction to chastise him. If the question were to arise, to what extent the demoniacal is a psychological problem, I must reply that the demoniacal is a state. Out of this state the particular sinful act can break forth perpetually. But the state is a possibility, although again in relation to freedom it is a reality posited by the qualitative leap.

The demoniacal is dread of the good. In the state of innocence freedom was not posited as freedom, its possibility appears in the dread of the individuality. In the demoniacal the situation is reversed. Freedom is posited as unfreedom, for freedom is lost. The possibility of freedom is in turn dread. The difference is absolute; for the possibility of freedom manifests itself here in relation to unfreedom, which is exactly the opposite of innocence, which is a determinant oriented towards freedom.

The demoniacal is unfreedom which would shut itself off. This, however, is an impossibility; it always maintains a relationship, and even when this has apparently disappeared it is nevertheless there, and dread manifests itself at once in the instant of contact with the good (cf. what was said above about the accounts in the New Testament).

The demoniacal is *shut-upness* [*det Indesluttede*, or *Indesluttedhed*] *unfreely revealed*. These two traits denote, as they should, the same thing; for the shut-up is precisely the mute, and if it has to express itself, this must come about against its will when the freedom lying prone in unfreedom revolts upon coming into communication with freedom outside and now betrays unfreedom in such a way that it is the individual who betrays himself against his will in dread. The word "shut-up" must therefore be taken here in a perfectly definite sense, for in the sense of reserve, in which it is commonly used,[12] it may denote the highest freedom. Brutus, Henry V of England as Prince of Wales, etc., were in this sense shut-up until the time came when it was evident that their shut-upness was a pact with the good. Such a shut-upness was therefore identical with expansion, and never is there an individuality which in the finer and nobler sense of the word is more expanded than he who is shut-up within the womb of a great idea. Freedom is precisely the expansive. It is in opposition to this I would employ the word "shut-up," κατ' ἐξοχήν, for "unfreedom." Commonly a more metaphysical term is used for the evil. It is called "negating." The ethical term precisely corresponding to that, when one contemplates the effect thereof upon the individual, is shut-upness. The demoniacal does not shut itself up *with* something, but shuts *itself* up; and in this lies the mystery of existence, the fact that unfreedom makes a prisoner precisely of itself. Freedom is constantly communicating (it will do no harm to take into account even the religious significance of this word[13]); unfreedom becomes more and more shut-up and wants no communication. This can be observed in all spheres. It shows itself in hypochondriacs, in crotcheteers, it shows itself in the highest passions when by a profound misunderstanding they introduce silence as a system.* When freedom then comes in contact with

---

* Already it has been said, and it is affirmed here again, that the demoniacal has a much greater amplitude than one commonly believes. In the preceding section the formations were indicated which point in another direction, and here

shut-upness it becomes afraid [*angest*]. In common speech we have an expression which is exceedingly suggestive. We say of a person that he will not come out with it. The shut-up is precisely the mute; the spoken word is precisely the saving thing, that which delivers from the mute abstraction of the shut-up. Let the demoniacal here mean x; freedom's relation to it from without, x: the law for the revelation of the demoniacal is that against its will it comes out with it. For by speech is implied a communication. A demoniac in the New Testament says therefore to Christ, τί ἐμοὶ καὶ σοί[14]; he goes on to say that Christ has come to destroy him (dread of the good). Or a demoniac beseeches Christ to go another way.[15] (When dread is dread of the evil, cf. §1, the individual seeks refuge in salvation.)

Life presents examples of this abundantly in all possible spheres and in all possible degrees. A hardened criminal will not go to confession (the demoniacal consists precisely in this, that the man is not willing to communicate with the good through the chastisement of suffering). There is a method applicable to such a case which perhaps is rarely used: it is silence and the power of the eye. If an inquisitor has the requisite physical strength and spiritual elasticity to hold out, though it were for sixteen hours, he will at last be rewarded by the admission breaking out involuntarily. No man who has a bad conscience can endure silence. Put him in solitary confinement, and he will become apathetic. But this silence, while the judge is present, and the clerk waiting to inscribe the confession in the record, is the most searching interrogation and the most terrible torture, and yet lawful; but it is by no means so easy to bring this about as one may suppose. The only power which can compel shut-upness to speak is either a higher demon (for every devil has his turn to reign) or the good which is absolutely able to be silent. And if here in this examination by silence any artfulness would put the man in embarrassment, the inquisitor himself will become ashamed, and it will prove that he at last becomes afraid of himself and must break the silence. Confronted with a subordinate demon, or with subordinate human beings whose God-consciousness is not strongly developed, shut-up-

there follows the second suite of formations, and as I have represented the matter this distinction can be carried out. If anyone has a better division to offer, let it be preferred. But it is not a bad thing to be a little cautious in these domains, for otherwise everything coagulates.

ness triumphs absolutely, because the former is not able to hold
out, and the latter, in all innocence, are accustomed to live from
hand to mouth and keep the heart on the tongue. It is incredible
what power resolute reserve is capable of exercising over such
men, how they end by begging and imploring for merely one
word to break the stillness, but it is also shocking to crush the
weak under foot in this fashion. It may be thought perhaps that
such things occur only among princes and Jesuits, that to get
a clear notion of it one must think of Domitian, Cromwell, the
Duke of Alba, or a general of the Jesuit Order, which is almost
an appellative term for this. Not at all, it occurs much more frequently. However, one must be cautious in passing judgment
upon the phenomenon; for, although the phenomenon is the same,
the reason for it may be exactly the opposite, since the individual who subjects others to the despotism and torture of shut-
upness might himself wish to speak, might himself be waiting for
a higher demon who could bring the revelation forth. But the
torturer may also be selfishly related to his shut-upness. But about
this I could write a whole book, in spite of the fact that I have
not (after the custom and established convention of observers in
our age) been either in Paris or London—as if there was such a
lot to be learned there besides talk and the wisdom of traveling
salesmen. If only one pays attention to oneself, an observer will
with five men, five women, and ten children have enough for the
discovery of all possible states of the human soul. What I should
have to say in such a book would have some importance, especially
for everyone who has to deal with children or has any relation with
them. It is of infinite importance that a child be brought up with
a conception of the lofty shut-upness [reserve], and be saved from
the mistaken kind. In an external respect it is easy to perceive when
the moment has arrived that one ought to let the child walk alone;
in a spiritual respect it is not so easy. In a spiritual respect the
problem is very difficult, and one cannot exempt oneself from responsibility by keeping a nursemaid and buying a gocart. The art
is to be constantly present and yet not to be present, to let the child
be allowed to develop itself, while nevertheless one has constantly
a survey clearly before one. The art is to leave the child to itself
in the very highest measure and on the greatest possible scale, and
to express this apparent abandonment in such a way that, unob-
served, one at the same time knows everything. One can quite well
find time for this even if one is a royal functionary. If only one

will, one can do everything. And the father who educates or does everything for the child entrusted to him, but has not prevented him from becoming shut-up, has incurred a great accountability.

The demoniacal is the shut-up, the demoniacal is dread of the good. We will now let the shut-up be X, an unknown quantity, and let its content too be X, which may denote the most terrible thing or the most insignificant, the most appalling thing, the presence of which in life is perhaps not dreamt of by many, or the bagatelle to which nobody pays any attention.* What then may be the significance of the good regarded as an X? It signifies revelation.† Revelation may in turn signify the sublimest thing (redemption in the most eminent sense) and the most insignificant (the utterance of a casual remark)—this must not disturb us, the category remains the same. The phenomena have this in common, that they are demoniacal, even though the differences are dizzy ones. "Revelation" in this context is the good, for revelation is the first utterance of salvation. Here applies the old saying, that if one dare utter the word, the enchantment of the magic spell is broken, and hence it is that the somnambulist wakes when his name is called.

The collisions of shut-upness in connection with revelation may in turn be infinitely various, with countless nuances, for the vegetative luxuriance of the spiritual life does not fall short of that in nature, and the spiritual states are more countless in their diversity than are the flowers. Shut-upness may wish for revelation, wish that it might be effected from without, that this might happen to it. (This is a misunderstanding, since it is a womanish relation to the freedom posited in revelation and to the freedom which posits revelation. Unfreedom may very well remain even though the state of the shut-up becomes happier.) It may will revelation

* To be able to use its category is a *conditio sine qua non* if observation is in a deeper sense to have significance. When the phenomenon is present to a certain degree most men notice it but are not able to explain it because they lack the category, whereas if they had it, they would have a key which opens the door wherever there is a trace of the phenomenon; for when they are under the category the phenomena are obedient to it just as the spirit of the ring obeys the ring.

† I have used the word "revelation" deliberately. Here I might have called the good "transparency." If I had reason to fear that anyone could misunderstand the word "revelation" and the exposition of its relation to the demoniacal, as though I were constantly speaking of something external, a tangible confession made public, which in so far as it is external is not apt for our purpose—then I would have chosen another word.

to a certain degree, but keep back a little vestige, only to begin all over again with shut-upness. (This is the case with subordinate natures which can do nothing *en gros*.) It may will revelation, but *incognito*. (This is the most subtle contradiction of shut-upness. Nevertheless, examples of it are to be found in poetic existences.[16]) Revelation may have already conquered, shut-upness ventures to employ its last expedient and is cunning enough to transform revelation itself into a mystification, and shut-upness has won.*

But I dare not continue. How could I ever finish if I were merely to indicate these states algebraically, not to speak of describing them, or if I would break the silence of shut-upness in order to let its monologues become audible? For its talk is precisely monologue, and hence when we would characterize a shut-up we say that he talks to himself. But here I essay only to give everything "an understanding but no tongue," as said the shut-up Hamlet warningly to his two friends.[17]

However, I will indicate one collision, the contradiction of which is as terrible as is shut-upness itself. What the shut-up keeps hidden in his close reserve may be so terrible that he dare not utter it even in his own hearing, because it seems to him as though by this very utterance he were committing a new sin, or as though it would tempt him again. In order that this phenomenon may occur the individual must be such a blending of purity and impurity as seldom is encountered. It is therefore most likely to occur when the individual at the time of accomplishing the terrible act was not master of himself. For example, a man in a state of intoxication may have done what he remembers only obscurely, yet knows that it was so wild a thing that it is almost impossible for him to recognize himself. The same may also be the case with a man who once was insane and has retained a memory of that previous state. What decides whether the phenomenon is demoniacal is the attitude of the individual towards revelation, whether he is willing to permeate that fact with freedom, assume the responsibility of it in freedom. If he is not willing to do that, then the phenomenon is demoniacal. This distinction must be held sharply, for even the

* It is easy to see that shut-upness *eo ipso* signifies a lie, or, if you prefer, untruth. But untruth is precisely unfreedom, it is dread of revelation. Hence the devil is called the father of lies. That there is a great difference between a lie and an untruth, between lies and lies, and between untruth and untruth, I have always conceded, but the category is the same.

man who merely wishes revelation is nevertheless essentially demoniacal. He has in fact two wills, one of them subordinate, impotent,
which wills revelation, and a stronger will which wills to be shut
up; but the fact that this is the stronger shows that essentially he
is demoniacal. Close reserve is involuntary revelation. The weaker
the individuality originally is, or in proportion as the elasticity of
freedom is consumed in the service of close reserve, the more certainly will the secret break out at last. The most trivial contact,
a glance in passing, etc., is sufficient to start that terrible monologue; or it may be comical, depending upon the content of the
close reserve. The ventriloquism may be plainly declarative, or it
may be indirect, as when an insane man points to another person
and says, "He is very objectionable to me, he's probably insane."
Revelation may declare itself in words when the unfortunate man
ends by intruding upon everyone his hidden secret. It may declare
itself by a look, by a glance; for there is a glance of the eye by
which a man involuntarily reveals what is hidden. There is an ac-
cusing glance which reveals what one almost dreads to understand;
a contrite, imploring glance which hardly tempts curiosity to peer
into this involuntary telegraphy. Depending upon the content of close
reserve, all this in turn may be almost comical, when what dread reveals against its will are ludicrous incidents, pettiness, vanity,
pranks, petty envy, little crotchets about medicine and health, etc.

The demoniacal is the sudden. The sudden is a new expression
for close reserve seen in another aspect. The demoniacal is characterized as the shut-up when one reflects upon the content, it is
characterized as the sudden when one reflects upon time. Close
reserve was the effect of the negating retrenchment of the ego in
the individuality. Reservedness closed itself constantly more and
more against communication. But communication is in turn the
expression for continuity, and the negation of continuity is the
sudden. One might suppose that close reserve would have an extraordinary continuity. But exactly the opposite is the case, although in comparison with the soft and vapid dispersion of oneself
which ends with the sense impression, this has an appearance of
continuity. The continuity which close reserve may have can be
compared with the vertigo we may suppose a top must feel as
it revolves perpetually upon its pivot. In case this close reserve
does not carry the thing so far as to become completely insane,
insanity being the pitiful *perpetuum mobile* of monotonous indif-

ference, the individuality will still retain a certain continuity with the rest of human life. Against the foil of this continuity, that apparent continuity of close reserve will display itself as the sudden. One instant it is there, the next it is gone, and no sooner is it gone than it is there again as large as life. It cannot be embroidered upon any continuity, nor woven into it, but what expresses itself thus is precisely the sudden.

In case the demoniacal were something somatic, there never would be the sudden. When a fever, insanity, etc., comes back again, one discovers at last a law, and this law in some degree annuls the sudden. But the sudden recognizes no law. It does not properly belong among natural phenomena but is psychic, is the expression of unfreedom.

Like the demoniacal, the sudden is dread of the good. The good in this context means continuity, for the first expression of salvation is continuity. While the life of the individual goes on in a certain degree in continuity with the rest of human life, close reserve maintains itself in him as continuity's abracadabra which communicates only with itself and therefore does not cease to be the sudden.

Depending upon the content of close reserve, the sudden may signify the terrible, but also, for the observer, the effect may appear comic. In this connection we must note that every individual has a little of this suddenness, just as every individual has a little bit of *l'idée fixe*.

I will not follow this out further, but to uphold my category I will recall the fact that the sudden is always due to dread of the good, because there is something which freedom is not willing to permeate. Among the formations which lie in dread of the evil it is weakness which corresponds to what we here call "the sudden."

If in a different way we would make clear to ourselves how it is the demoniacal is the sudden, we may from a purely aesthetic point of view consider the question how the demoniacal can best be represented on the stage. If one would present Mephistopheles, it is well enough to give him lines to recite, if one wishes to use him as an efficient force in the dramatic action, rather than depict his character properly. In that case Mephistopheles is not really represented but is vaguely indicated as a malicious, witty, intriguing pate. This is a volatilization which a popular legend has already improved upon. It recounts that the devil sat and speculated for 3000 years how to overthrow man—then finally he found it out. Here the accent is placed upon the 3000 years, and the picture this produces in the mind is precisely that of the brooding shut-upness of the demoniacal. If one would not volatilize Mephistopheles in the way above indicated, one may choose another mode of representation. In this it will appear that Mephistopheles is essentially mimic.* Even the terrible words which rise out of the abyss of malice are incapable of producing such an effect as does the suddenness of the leap which lies within the compass of mimic art. Even were the word more terrible, even though it were a Shakespeare, a Byron, a Shelley, that breaks the silence, the word always conserves its saving power; for even all despair and all the horror of evil expressed in one word is not so horrible as silence. Mimic art is able to express the sudden, though this does not imply that this art as such is the sudden. In this respect Bournonville as Master of the Ballet deserves great credit for his representation of Mephistopheles. The horror which seizes one on seeing Mephistopheles leap in through the window and remain stationary in the attitude of the leap! This bound within the leap, recalling the plunge of the bird of prey and the bound of the wild beast, which are doubly terrifying because commonly they break forth from complete immobility, produces therefore an infinite impression. Hence Mephistopheles must walk as little as possible, for the walk itself is in a way a transition to the leap, suggests a presentiment of its possibility. This first appearance of Mephistopheles in the ballet of *Faust* is not a *coup de théâtre* but a very profound thought. Words and speech, short as they may be, have yet always, if we regard the thing abstractly, a certain continuity, because it is in time they are heard. But the sudden is completely detached from continuity, whether it be with the past or with the future. So it is with Mephistopheles. No one has yet seen him—when there he stands, wholly himself from head to feet, and speed cannot be expressed more strongly than by the fact that he stands

* The author of *Either/Or* has called attention to the fact that Don Juan is essentially musical. Precisely in the same sense it is true of Mephistopheles that he is essentially mimic. Theatrical art has suffered the same fate as music: it has been supposed that everything could become theatrical and everything musical. We have a ballet, it is called *Faust*. If the composer had really understood what is implied by interpreting *Faust* mimically, it never would have occurred to him to turn *Faust* into a ballet.

there with one leap. If this passes into a walk, the effect is weakened. By the fact that Mephistopheles is represented in this fashion, his appearance upon the scene produces the effect of the demoniacal, which comes more suddenly than the thief in the night, for one commonly thinks of the thief as moving stealthily. By this then Mephistopheles reveals his nature, which, like the demoniacal nature, is the sudden. Thus in its forward movement the demoniacal is the sudden, thus it springs into existence in a man, and thus man himself is sudden in so far as he is demoniacal, whether it be that this power has possessed him wholly or that only a little part of it is present in him. Thus the demoniacal always is, and thus suddenly does unfreedom become dread, and such too is the movement of its dread. Hence the aptness of the demoniacal for the mimic art, not in the sense of the beautiful but of the sudden, the abrupt, something which life often gives us opportunity to observe.

The demoniacal is the vacuous, the tedious. Having called attention, apropos of the sudden, to the aesthetic problem of how to represent the demoniacal on the stage, I will raise the same question again in order to throw light upon the affirmation I have made here. When a demon is allowed to speak, and there is someone then who would impersonate him, the actor who has such a problem to solve must be clear about the categories. He knows that the demoniacal is essentially mimic; the sudden, however, is not attainable because that would interrupt the lines. So he will not botch the thing, with the notion that by blurting out the words, etc., he might be capable of producing any genuine effect. Therefore he rightly chooses exactly the opposite, namely, the tedious. The continuity which corresponds to the sudden is what one might call "extinction." Tediousness, the impression of being extinct, is in fact a continuity in nothingness. Now we can interpret a little differently the figure stated in the popular legend. The 3000 years are not now stressed in order to emphasize the sudden, but this prodigious space of time calls forth an apprehension of the horrible emptiness and vacuity of the evil. Freedom is quietness in continuity; the opposite of this is the sudden, but it may also be the quiet which invariably comes to mind when we see a man who looks as if he had been long dead and buried.) An actor who understands this will also see that in finding out how the demoniacal can be impersonated he has found at the same time an expression for the comical. The comical effect can be produced in exactly the same way. In fact, when all ethical determinants are put to one side and one employs only the metaphysical determinants of emptiness, we have the trivial, from which one can easily derive a comical effect.*

The vacuous or the tedious characterize in turn shut-upness. When I dwelt upon the significance of the sudden, the category of shut-upness reflected upon the content. Now when I take into account the vacuous, the tedious, this in turn reflects upon the content, and shut-upness indicates the form which corresponds to this content. Thus the whole definition of this concept is rounded out, for the form of vacuity is precisely shut-upness. It must be constantly remembered that according to my terminology one cannot be shut up in God or in the good, for this kind of reserve is precisely the utmost expansion. The more definitely conscience is in this way developed in a man, the more he is expanded, even though in other respects he shuts himself off from the whole world.

If I were now disposed to call to mind the new philosophical terminology, I might say that the demoniacal is "the negative" or "nothing," like the fairies, which are empty silhouettes. However, I am not inclined to do so. This terminology has become so amiable and pliable by moving much in society that it can signify whatever you will. "The negative," if I were to use this term, would signify the form of "nothing," just as the vacuous corresponds to shut-upness. But "the negative" has the defect of being defined rather from the outside, by reference to the other thing which is negated, whereas the category shut-up exactly defines the state.

If "the negative" is conceived in this way, I have no objection to its being used to denote the demoniacal, provided "the negative" will be able to rid itself of all the crochets modern philosophy has put into its head. "The negative" has gradually become a figure

---

* Little Winsløv's[18] impersonation of Klister in *The Inseparables* was so profound because he had rightly comprehended the tedious as the comical. That a loving attachment, which when it exists in truth possesses the content of continuity, is exactly the opposite, viz. an infinite emptiness, not because Klister is a bad man, unfaithful, etc., since on the contrary he is sincerely in love, but because here again he is a supernumerary volunteer just as in the custom house —such an attachment, I say, has a highly comic effect, if one puts the accent precisely upon the tedious. Klister's position in the custom house can only in an unjustifiable way be conceived as comic; for, good Lord, can Klister help it that there was no promotion to be had?—but in relation to his love, after all, he is his own master.

for vaudeville, and this word always makes me smile, just as one smiles when in real life or in the songs of Bellmann,[19] for example, one comes across one of those droll characters who first was a trumpeter, later became commissary officer, then innkeeper, then in turn letter-carrier, etc. Thus irony has been explained as the negative. The first discoverer of this explanation was Hegel,[20] who, strangely enough, had no great sense for irony. That it was Socrates who introduced irony into the world and gave the baby its name, that his irony was precisely the close reserve which began by shutting himself off from men, by shutting himself in with himself in order to be expanded in the Deity, began by shutting his door against men and making jest of those who stood outside, in order to talk in secret—who troubles himself about that?

Apropos of one or another casual phenomenon somebody comes out with this word—and so it must be irony. Then come the "parrots," who, in spite of their broad survey of universal history, which unfortunately is totally lacking in contemplation, know just as much about concepts as that egregious youth knew about raisins, who when he appeared as candidate for the position of grocer's clerk and was asked where raisins came from, replied ingenuously, "We get ours from Pedersen's grocery in Cross Street."

We now return again to the definition that the demoniacal is dread of the good. In case unfreedom were, on the one hand, capable of completely shutting itself off and hypostatizing itself, and, on the other hand, in case it did not constantly will to do so* (herein is the contradiction that unfreedom wills something when precisely it has lost will), then the demoniacal would not be dread of the good. For this cause also dread manifests itself clearly at the instant of contact with the good. Whether the demoniacal in the particular individual signifies the terrible, or whether evil is present only like a spot on the sun or like the little white dot in

---

* This we must constantly hold fast, in spite of demoniacal and linguistic illusions which to describe this state use such expressions that one is almost tempted to forget that unfreedom is a phenomenon of freedom and is not to be explained by naturalistic categories. Even when unfreedom affirms in the strongest terms that it does not will itself, this is an untruth, for in unfreedom there is constantly a will which is stronger than the wish. The situation may be exceedingly deceptive, but one can bring such a man to despair by holding out and keeping one's categories pure in opposition to his sophisms. One ought not to be apprehensive for oneself in this situation, but neither should youthful experimenters try their hand in these spheres.

the corn, the total demoniacal and the partial demoniacal have the same characteristics, and the tiny little bit is dread of the good in the same sense as is that which is totally beset by evil. The bondage of sin is also of course unfreedom; but, as was expounded above, its direction is a different one, it is dread of the evil. If we do not hold fast to this, it will not be possible to explain anything.

Unfreedom, the demoniacal, is therefore a state. Thus it is psychology regards it. Ethics, on the other hand, sees how out of it there constantly springs the new sin; for only the good is unity of state and movement.

Freedom, however, may be lost in various ways, and so also may the demoniacal be of various sorts. This variety I will now consider under the following rubrics: freedom lost somatic-psychically; freedom lost pneumatically. From the foregoing the reader must be familiar with the fact that I use the term "demoniacal" in a very wide sense, yet without stretching it further, be it noted, than the concept will reach. It doesn't do much good to make the demoniacal a great horned owl at which one shudders horribly and thereupon puts it out of mind with the reflection that it is many centuries since it was seen in the world. This assumption is a great piece of foolishness, for it has perhaps never been so widespread as in our times, only that nowadays it shows itself especially in spiritual or intellectual spheres.

A. FREEDOM LOST SOMATIC-PSYCHICALLY

It is not my purpose here to make a pompous display of philosophical deliberations about the relation subsisting between soul and body, to discuss in what sense the soul itself produces its body (whether this be understood in the Greek or in the German way), in what sense freedom itself (to recall an expression of Schelling's[21]) by an act of "corporization" posits its own body. Nothing of that sort is needed here; it is enough for my purpose if to the best of my poor ability I express myself by saying that the body is an organ of the soul, and thus in turn of the spirit. So soon as the subordinate relationship comes to an end, so soon as the body revolts, so soon as freedom enters into a conspiracy with it against itself, there unfreedom is present as the demoniacal. Inasmuch as there may be someone who has not yet apprehended sharply the difference between what is set forth in this section and what was explained earlier, I will here state it again. In case freedom does not go over to the camp of rebellion, there will be present the dread of revolution, but as dread of the evil, not as dread of the good.

It will now be easily seen what a countless multiplicity of nuances is comprehended by the demoniacal in these spheres, some of them so infinitesimal that they are visible only to microscopic observation, and some so dialectic that one must have great flexibility in the use of one's category to see that these nuances belong under it: an exaggerated sensibility, an exaggerated irritability, nervous affections, hysteria, hypochondria, etc., are all of them nuances of it, or may be. This makes it so difficult to talk of the subject *in abstracto*, since the talk becomes algebraical. However, I can do no more here.

The utmost extreme in this sphere is, as also it commonly is called, bestial perdition. In this state the demoniacal evinces itself in the fact that, like that demoniac in the New Testament, it says τί ἐμοὶ καὶ σοί.²² It shuns therefore every contact with the good, whether this actually threatens it by wanting to help it to freedom, or merely touches it quite casually. Even this is enough, for dread is extraordinarily quick. Hence one hears quite commonly from such a demoniac a rejoinder which contains in it all the horror of this state: "Let me be the miserable man I am," or when one hears such a man say, when he is speaking of a definite moment in his past life, "At that time perhaps I might have been saved," which is the most terrible line that could be put in a man's mouth. It is not punishment, not thunderous words of reproof, which put him in dread; on the contrary, it is every word which would put itself in relation to the freedom scuttled and sunk in unfreedom. In this phenomenon dread expresses itself also in another way. Among such demoniacs one finds a cohesion in which they cling together with so much dread and so indissolubly that no friendship matches it in heartiness. The French physician Duchatelet adduces examples of this in his treatise. And this sociability of dread will show itself everywhere in this sphere. The sociability by itself furnishes assurance that the demoniacal is present, for in so far as one finds an analogous situation as an expression of the bondage of sin, sociability is not in evidence, because the dread is that of the evil.

I do not wish to follow this out further. My prime interest at this point is to have my classification in good order.

B. FREEDOM LOST PNEUMATICALLY

(a). *General observations.* This formation of the demoniacal is very widespread, and here diverse phenomena are encountered. The demoniacal does not of course depend upon the diversity of intellectual content but upon the relation of freedom to the given content,* and to the possible content in proportion to the intellectuality, the demoniacal being able to express itself as indolence, putting the thing off till another time, as curiosity which comes to nothing more than curiosity, as dishonest self-deception, as effeminate softness which relies upon others, as an affectation of aristocratic indifference, as stupid bustle, etc.

The content of freedom, intellectually regarded, is the truth which makes man free. But precisely for this reason is truth in such a sense the work of freedom that it is constantly engaged in producing truth. It is a matter of course that I am not thinking here of the clever conceit of modern philosophy[23] that the necessity of thought is also its liberty, which therefore when it talks of liberty of thought is only talking about the eternal immanent movement of thought. Such a conceit serves only to confuse, and to make more difficult communication between men. What I am talking about, on the other hand, is something quite simple and plain, that truth exists for the particular individual only as he himself produces it in action. If truth exists for him in any other way, and is prevented from existing for him in that way, we have there a phenomenon of the demoniacal. Truth has always had many loud preachers, but the question is whether a man is willing in the deepest sense to recognize truth, to let it permeate his whole being, to assume all the consequences of it, and not to keep in case of need a hiding place for himself, and a Judas-kiss as the consequence.

In modern times there has been talk enough about truth; now it is high time for certitude, inwardness, to be asserted, not in the abstract sense in which Fichte employed this word,[24] but in a perfectly concrete sense.

Certitude, inwardness, which can only be attained by and exist

---

* In the New Testament we find the expression σοφία δαιμονιώδης (James 3:15). In the way it is described in this passage the category is not clear. But on the other hand when one takes account of the passage in 2:19, καὶ τὰ δαιμόνια πιστεύουσιν καὶ φρίσσουσιν, one sees precisely in the demoniacal knowledge the relation of unfreedom to the knowledge here posited.

in action, determines whether the individual is demoniacal or not. One has only to hold the category fast, then everything gives way, and it becomes clear, for example, that willfulness, unbelief, mockery of religion, etc., are not, as is commonly believed, lacking in content, but evince lack of certitude, exactly in the same sense as does superstition, servility, devoteeism. The negative phenomena lack certitude precisely because they dread the content.

I have no desire to speak in strong terms about this age as a whole, but he who has observed the contemporary generation will surely not deny that the incongruity in it and the reason for its dread and restlessness is this, that in one direction truth increases in extent, in mass, partly also in abstract clarity, whereas certitude steadily decreases. What extraordinary metaphysical and logical efforts have been made to furnish a new and exhaustive proof of the immortality of the soul, an unimpeachable proof which would combine all other proofs; and curiously enough, while this is going on certitude decreases! The thought of immortality has a power and pith in its consequences, an implication of responsibility in the acceptance of it, which perhaps would transform the whole life in a way which one fears. One saves oneself, therefore, and tranquilizes one's soul by exerting one's mind in order to produce a new proof. What is a proof like that but a "good work" in the Catholic sense? Every such individual who knows how to produce a new proof of the immortality of the soul (to stick to this illustration), but is not himself convinced, will always be in dread of every phenomenon which forces upon him a more penetrating understanding of what is meant by saying that a man is immortal. It will disturb the man, he will feel uncomfortably affected when a perfectly simple man talks quite simply about immortality.—In an opposite direction inwardness may be lacking. A partisan of the most rigid orthodoxy may be demoniacal. He knows it all, he bows before the holy, truth is for him an ensemble of ceremonies, he talks about presenting himself before the throne of God, of how many times one must bow, he knows everything the same way as does the pupil who is able to demonstrate a mathematical proposition with the letters ABC, but not when they are changed to DEF. He is therefore in dread whenever he hears something not arranged in the same order. And yet how closely he resembles a modern speculative philosopher who found out a new proof for the immortality of the soul, then came into mortal

danger and could not produce his proof because he ha
notebooks with him. And what is it both of them lack? Certitude.—
Superstition and unbelief are both of them forms of unfreedom.
In superstition there is conceded to objectivity a power like that
of Medusa's head to turn subjectivity to stone, and unfreedom
does not will to have the spell broken. The highest and apparently
the freest expression of unbelief is mockery. But certitude is
precisely what mockery lacks, therefore it mocks. But the mockery
of so many mockers, if only one could look into it, would recall
that dread of the demoniac who cried, τί ἐμοὶ καὶ σοί. It is therefore a curious phenomenon that there are perhaps few men so
vain and so jealous of the applause of the instant as is a mocker.

With what industrious zeal, with what sacrifice of time, of
diligence, of writing materials, the speculative philosophers in
our time have labored to get a strong and complete proof of the
existence of God! But in the same degree that the excellence of
the proof increases, certitude seems to decrease. The thought of
the existence of a God, so soon as it is placed as such before the
freedom of the individual, has an omnipresence which for the
sensitive individual has something embarrassing about it, even
if one does not want to behave badly. And in truth it requires
inwardness to live a common life on beautiful and affectionate
terms with this conception, it is a tour de force even greater than
being a model husband. Therefore how uncomfortably such an
individuality may be affected upon hearing perfectly naïve and
simple people talk about God's existence. The demonstration of
God's existence is something one may occasionally be engaged in,
learnedly and metaphysically, but the thought of God would intrude on every occasion. What is it such an individuality lacks?
Inwardness.—Also in an opposite direction inwardness may be
lacking. The so-called saints are often the object of the world's
mockery. They themselves explain this by the consideration that
the world is evil. This, however, is not the whole truth. When
the "saint" is unfree with respect to his piety, i.e. lacks inwardness, he is, as seen from a purely aesthetic point of view, simply
comic. To that extent the world is justified in laughing at him.
In case a bow-legged man desired to act as dancing-master, without being able to execute a single step, he is comic. So it is too with
the religious. One sometimes hears such a saint beat time as it were
all by himself, exactly like one who cannot dance and yet knows

enough to beat time, though he never succeeds in getting in step. So the "saint" knows that the religious is absolutely commensurable, that the religious is not something which belongs to certain occasions and instants, but that a man always can have it with him. But when he essays to make it commensurable, he is not free, and one notices how he is beating time softly by himself, and one sees how nevertheless he is out of time with the measure and comes in wrong with his heavenly glance and folded hands, etc. For this reason such an individuality is so much in dread of everyone who has not had this coaching that to fortify itself it must grasp at these supercilious reflections about the world hating the pious.

Certitude, inwardness, is indeed subjectivity, but not in an entirely abstract sense. In general it is the misfortune of the newest knowledge that it is so terribly supercilious. The abstract subjectivity is just as uncertain and just as much lacking in inwardness as is the abstract objectivity. When one talks of it *in abstracto* one cannot see this, and in that case it is correct to say that the abstract subjectivity lacks content. When one speaks of it *in concreto* the content clearly appears, for the individuality which would turn itself into an abstraction lacks inwardness precisely as does the individuality which turns itself into a mere master of ceremonies.

(b). *The* Schema *for the exclusion or the lack of inwardness.* The lack [non-presence] of inwardness is always a consequence of reflection; accordingly every form will be a double form. One may perhaps be the less inclined to perceive this for the reason that the spirit is commonly defined in perfectly abstract terms. It is customary to contrast immediacy and reflection (inwardness), and then comes the synthesis (or substantiality, subjectivity, identity—though they may call this identity "reason," "idea," "spirit"). But in the sphere of reality this is not true. There immediacy is also the immediacy of inwardness. The lack of inwardness is therefore in the first instance due to reflection.

Every form of the lack of inwardness is either activity-passivity or passivity-activity, and whether it be the one or the other is determined by self-reflection. The form itself runs through a considerable range of nuances in proportion as inwardness becomes more and more concrete. To understand and to understand are two things, is an old saying and a true one. Inwardness is an understanding, but *in concreto* the question is how this understanding is to be understood. To understand a speech is one thing, to understand the deitikose[25] implied in it is another; it is one thing for a man to understand what he himself says, to understand himself in what he says is another thing. The more concrete the content of consciousness is, the more concrete is the understanding, and when this understanding is lacking to consciousness we have a phenomenon of unfreedom which would shut itself off against freedom. If we take for example a fairly concrete religious consciousness which at the same time contains also a historical factor, understanding must have relation to that factor. In this example we can discover the two analogous forms of the demoniacal as they appear in this particular case. Thus when a rigidly orthodox man employs all his diligence and learning to prove that every word in the New Testament derives from the Apostle in question, inwardness then disappears little by little and gives place to understanding something quite different from what the man wished to understand. When a Freethinker employs all his acumen to show that the New Testament was not written until the second century, in that case it is precisely inwardness he is in fear of, and therefore he must have the New Testament put in the same class with all other books.* The most concrete content consciousness can have is consciousness of itself, not the pure self-con-

---

* Moreover, in the religious sphere the demoniacal may have a deceptive resemblance to the assault of doubt [*Anfægtelse*]. Its true nature can never be determined *in abstracto*. For example, a pious Christian believer may fall into the dread of being fearful of taking Communion. This is an assault of doubt —or rather, whether it is such will be shown by his attitude to the dread. On the other hand, a demoniacal nature may have gone so far, his religious consciousness may have become so concrete, that the inwardness of which he is in dread, and from the dread of which he tries to flee, is the purely personal understanding of the sacramental understanding. Only up to a certain point is he willing to go along with this understanding, there he breaks away and desires to maintain only an intellectual attitude, desires in one way or another to become more than the empirical, historically determined, finite individuality he is. He who is exposed to the assault of doubt wills to go on to that from which the assault of doubt would keep him away; where as the demoniacal himself wills to be away, in accord with his stronger will (that of unfreedom), while a weaker will in him wills to go on to that point. To this consideration one must hold fast, for otherwise one goes on to think of the demoniacal as so abstract that no such thing has ever been met with—as though the will of unfreedom were constituted as such [i.e. were the whole reality] and the will of freedom were not constantly present, weak as it may be, in self-contradiction.—If anyone desires material concerning the temptations of religious doubts and scruples, he will find it superabundantly in Görres' work on *Mysticism*.[26] However, I admit honestly that I have never had the courage to read it through, it is so full of dread. Yet this much I can perceive, that he has not always known how to discriminate between the demoniacal and the assaults of temptation, and hence he must be read with caution.

sciousness, but the self-consciousness which is so concrete that no author—not the most copious in his command of words, not the most consummate delineator of character—has ever been able to describe such a thing, although such a thing is what every man is. This self-consciousness is not contemplation; he who thinks that it is has not understood himself, for he sees that he himself is meanwhile in the process of becoming and so cannot be a finished product as the object of contemplation. This self-consciousness therefore is a deed, and this deed in turn is inwardness, and every time inwardness does not correspond to this consciousness, there is a form of the demoniacal as soon as the absence of inwardness expresses itself as dread of its acquisition.

In case the absence of inwardness were brought about by mechanical means, it would be a waste of time to talk about it. But this is not so, and therefore in every phenomenon of the absence of inwardness there is an activity, even if it has its beginning in passivity. The phenomena which begin in activity are more striking, therefore one sees them more easily, then forgets that in this activity there is manifested in turn a passivity and does not take into account the opposite phenomenon when talking about the demoniacal.

I will now glance at a few examples to show that the *schema* is correct.

Incredulity—superstition. They correspond to one another perfectly: both lack inwardness, but incredulity is passive through an activity, and superstition active through a passivity; the one, if you will, is more masculine, the other more feminine; and the content of both is reflection upon oneself. Essentially regarded, they are completely identical. Incredulity and superstition are both of them dread of faith; but incredulity begins in the activity of unfreedom, superstition begins in the passivity of unfreedom. Commonly one has in mind only the passivity of superstition, consequently it seems less distinguished or more excusable, depending upon whether aesthetico-ethical or ethical categories are applied. In superstition there is a weakness which deceives, but surely there must always be enough activity in it to support its passivity. Superstition is incredulous of itself, incredulity is superstitious in its regard for itself. The content of both is self-reflection [i.e. reflection upon oneself]. The indolence, cowardice and pusillanimity of superstition find it more comfortable to remain in it than to give it up; the defiance, pride, and arrogance of incredulity find it a hardier attitude to remain in it than to give it up.

The most refined form of such self-reflection is always that which becomes interesting to oneself by wishing oneself out of this state while nevertheless one remains complacently in it.

Hypocrisy—offense at the religious. These correspond to one another. Hypocrisy begins through an activity, offense through a passivity. Commonly, offense is judged more mildly, but if the individual continues in it, there must after all be precisely enough activity to support the suffering involved in it and not be willing to give it up. There is a positive receptivity in offense (for a tree or a stone is not offended) which is made evident when the offense is removed. On the other hand, the passivity of offense finds it more comfortable and easy to go on sitting and let, as it were, the consequences of offense pile up at compound interest. Therefore hypocrisy is offense at oneself, offense is hypocrisy to oneself. Both lack inwardness and dare not come to themselves. Hence all hypocrisy ends by being hypocritical to oneself, because the hypocrite is offended at himself or is an offense to himself. Hence all offense, if it is not removed, ends in hypocrisy towards others, since the offended man, because of the vast activity by which he remains in offense, has made that original receptivity something different and therefore he must be hypocritical towards others. One may even encounter in real life the case of an offended individual who at last finds need of this offense as a fig leaf for what well might require a hypocritical cloak.

Pride—cowardice. Pride begins through an activity, cowardice through a passivity; in other respects they are identical, for in cowardice there is precisely enough activity to maintain the dread of the good. Pride is a profound cowardice, for it is cowardly enough not to be willing to understand what pride truly is. So soon as this understanding is forced upon it, it is cowardly, disintegrates like a squib, bursts like a bubble. Cowardice is a profound pride, for it is cowardly enough not to be willing to understand the requirement of even a misunderstood pride, but by cringing as it does it manifests its pride, and also it knows how to allege in its favor the fact that it has never suffered a defeat, and is therefore proud of the negative expression of pride—that it has never suffered any loss. One may also encounter in real life the case of a proud individuality which was cowardly enough never to venture anything, cowardly enough to make itself as small as possible, precisely for the sake of saving its pride. If one were to put in juxtaposition an active-proud and a passive-proud individuality, one would have opportunity, precisely at the instant when the former fell, to convince oneself how proud essentially the cowardly man was.*

(c). *What is certitude and inwardness?* It is not easy to give a definition of it. However, in this context I would say that it is seriousness. This is a word which everyone understands in a way, and yet strangely enough there are perhaps not many words upon which men more rarely reflect. When Macbeth had murdered the King he cried:[27]

> From this instant
> There's nothing serious in mortality
> All is but toys: renown and grace is dead;
> The wine of life is drawn, and the mere lees
> Is left this vault to brag of.

It is true, Macbeth was a murderer, and therefore in his mouth these words ring with a note of truth which is terrible and harrowing, and yet everyone who has lost inwardness can with good reason say, "The wine of life is drawn," and can say too, "There's nothing serious in mortality, all is but toys"; for inwardness is precisely the fountain which springeth up unto eternal life, and what issues from this fountain is precisely seriousness. When Ecclesiastes says that all is vanity, it is precisely seriousness the preacher has *in mente*. On the other hand, when, after seriousness has been lost, it is said that all is vanity, this is only an active-passive expression of the fact (defiance characteristic of melancholy), or a passive-active (defiance characteristic of frivolity and mockery); here then is an occasion either to laugh or weep, but inwardness is lost.

So far as my knowledge extends, there exists no definition of

---

* In his treatise *De affectionibus*[28] Descartes calls attention to the fact that there is a passion corresponding to every other, except to the passion of wonder. His demonstration in detail is rather weak, but it is interesting to me that he made an exception of wonder, since, as everyone knows, this concept of wonder, according to both Plato and Aristotle,[29] is the passion of philosophy and the passion with which philosophy began. As a matter of fact, envy corresponds to wonder [in the sense of admiration], and modern philosophy would be inclined to talk of doubt as the opposite of wonder. Here precisely lies the fundamental error of modern philosophy, namely, that it wants to begin with the negative instead of with the positive, which always is the first, exactly as in affirming *omnis affirmatio est negatio* it is the *affirmatio* which is placed first. The question whether the positive or the negative is first is exceedingly important, and, so far as I know, the only modern philosopher who has pronounced in favor of the positive is Herbart.[30]

what seriousness is. I should be glad of this, if it be true; not because I am fond of the modern fluent way of thinking which has abolished definitions and lets everything coalesce, but because when it is a question of existential concepts it always is a sign of surer tact to abstain from definitions, because one does not like to construe in the form of a definition which so easily makes something else and something different out of a thought which essentially must be understood in a different fashion and which one has understood differently and has loved in an entirely different way. The man who really loves can hardly find pleasure and satisfaction, not to say increase of love, by busying himself with a definition of what love really is. The man who lives in daily and yet solemn familiarity with the thought that there is a God could hardly wish to spoil this thought for himself or to see it spoiled by piecing together a definition of what God is. So it is also with seriousness. It is so serious a matter that even to give a definition of it is frivolous. I do not say this, however, because my thought is vague, nor with the fear that some super-wise speculative philosopher might become suspicious of me as one who does not know what he is talking about—the sort of speculator who is as obstinate about the exposition of concepts as is the mathematician about proofs, and therefore would say, with regard to matters which cannot be reduced to logical concepts, as the mathematician says, "What does this prove?" To my mind, what I say here proves better than any exposition of concepts that I know seriously what the question is about.

Although I am not inclined to give a definition of seriousness or to talk about it with the jocosity of abstract thought, yet I will make some observations which may serve for orientation. In Rosenkrantz's *Psychology*[31] there is a definition* of *Gemüth*. He says on page 322 that *Gemüth* is a unity of feeling and self-con-

---

* I am always glad to assume that my reader has read just as much as I have. This assumption permits a great economy of time both for him who reads and for him who writes. So I assume that the reader knows this book. If such should not be the case, I counsel him to make himself acquainted with it, for it is really an able book, and if the author, who in other respects is distinguished for his sound sense and for his humane interest in human life, had been able to renounce the fanatical superstition he cherishes for an empty *schema*, he would sometimes have avoided being ridiculous. What he says in the text is for the most part very good, the only thing one now and again cannot understand is the pompous *schema* and how the perfectly concrete argument is relevant to it. (As an example I refer to pp. 209 ff., *Das Selbst—und das Selbst*: (1) *Der Tod*; (2) *Der Gegensatz von Herrschaft und Knechtschaft*.)

sciousness. In the exposition which precedes this he explains admirably *dass das Gefühl zum Selbstbewusstsein sich aufschliesse, und umgekehrt, dass der Inhalt des Selbstbewusstseins von dem Subject als der* seinige *gefühlt wird. Erst diese Einheit kann man Gemüth nennen. Denn fehlt die Klarheit der Erkenntniss, das Wissen vom Gefühl, so existirt nur der Drang des Naturgeistes, der Turgor der Unmittelbarkeit. Fehlt aber das Gefühl, so existirt nur ein abstracter Begriff, der nicht die letzte Innigkeit des geistigen Daseins erreicht hat, der nicht mit dem Selbst des Geistes Eines geworden ist* (cf. pp. 320 f.). When in turn one turns back and follows his definition of *Gefühl* as the spirit's *unmittelbare Einheit seiner Seelenhaftigkeit und seines Bewusstseins* (p. 242) and remembers that in the definition of *Seelenhaftigkeit* account has been taken of the unity with the immediate natural determinism, then when all this is taken together one has the conception of a concrete personality.

Now seriousness and *Gemüth* correspond in such a way that seriousness is a higher and deeper expression for what *Gemüth* is. *Gemüth* is a determinant of immediacy, whereas seriousness is the acquired originality of *Gemüth*, conserved in the responsibility of freedom, and raised to a higher order (*aufgehoben*) in the enjoyment of blessedness. The originality of seriousness in the course of its historical development evinces precisely its eternal character, and for this cause seriousness can never become habit. Rosenkrantz deals with habit only in his chapter on phenomenology,[32] not under pneumatology; but habit belongs also under this heading, and habit arises as soon as the eternal goes out of repetition. When originality in seriousness is acquired and conserved, then there is succession and repetition; but when originality is lacking in repetition we have habit. The serious man is serious precisely through the originality with which he comes back in repetition. It is true that a lively and heartfelt feeling conserves this originality; but the heartiness of feeling is a fire which may cool when seriousness no longer supports it; and on the other hand the heartiness of feeling is uncertain in its moods, i.e. it is at one time more hearty than at another. To make everything as clear as possible I will illustrate this by an example. A clergyman has to recite every Sunday the prescribed prayer, or he has to baptize several children every Sunday. Now suppose he is enthusiastic, etc.—the fire goes out; he will thrill and move people, but at one time more, at another less. Only seriousness is capable of coming back regularly every Sunday with the same originality to the same thing.*

But this same thing to which seriousness must return with the same seriousness can only be seriousness itself, otherwise it becomes pedantry. In this sense seriousness means the personality itself, and only a serious personality is a real personality, and only a serious personality can do anything seriously, for to do something seriously one needs first of all to know what is the object to which seriousness is directed.

In common life there is a good deal of talk about seriousness: one man becomes serious about the national debt, another about the categories, a third about a performance at the theater, etc. Irony discovers that such is the case, and with that it has plenty to do, for everyone who becomes serious at the wrong place is *eo ipso* comic, even though our age and its opinions which are ridiculed as burlesque may be exceedingly serious about it all. There is therefore no safer measuring rod to determine what a man is essentially worth than that which he furnishes by his own loquacity or which one gets by cunningly extracting his secret as to what it was that made him serious in life. For though one may be born with a *Gemüth*, one is not born with seriousness. The phrase, "what made him serious in life," must of course be understood pregnantly as that from which in the deepest sense the individual dates his seriousness. For after having become truly serious about that which is the proper object of seriousness, one can very well treat various things seriously, if you care to say so, but the question is about how one first became serious about the proper object of seriousness. This object every man has, for it is *himself*, and he who did not become serious about this but about something else, something big and noisy, is in spite of all his seriousness... a wag, and though for a while he may deceive irony, he shall *deo volente* end by being comic, for irony is jealous in behalf of seriousness. He, on the other hand, who became serious at the right place will show his soundness of mind by being able to treat everything else just as well sentimentally as he does jocosely, even though the serious-minded buffoons feel cold shivers run down their

* It was in this sense that Constantine Constantius said in *Repetition* (p. 6), "Repetition is the seriousness of existence," and that it is not life's seriousness to be a royal equerry, even if such a man every time he mounted his horse were to do it with all possible seriousness.

spines at seeing this man make jest of that which makes them dreadfully serious. But with regard to the truly serious he will know how to tolerate no pleasantries, and if he forgets this, it will happen to him as it did to Albertus Magnus when he presumptuously plumed himself over against the Deity* and suddenly became stupid, it will happen to him as it did to Bellerophon, who sat tranquilly upon his Pegasus in the service of the idea, but fell when he wished to misuse Pegasus by riding to a rendezvous with an earthly woman.

Inwardness, certitude, is seriousness. This makes a pretty poor showing. If I had gone on to say that it is subjectivity, the pure subjectivity, the *übergreifende* subjectivity—that would have been saying something, something which would have made many people serious. However, I can also express what seriousness is in another way. If inwardness is lacking, the spirit is finitized. Inwardness is therefore eternity, or the determinant of the eternal in a man.

If then one would study the demoniacal to good purpose, one needs only to see how the eternal is conceived in the individuality, and at once one is thoroughly informed. In this respect our age offers a wide field for the observer. The eternal is frequently talked about, some rejecting it, others accepting it, and, considering the way it is done, the latter as well as the former evinces lack of in-

---

* Cf. Marbach, *Geschichte der Philosophie,* 2nd ed., p. 302, note: *Albertus repente ex asino factus philosophus et ex philosopho asinus.* Cf. Tennemann, Vol. 8, 2nd ed., p. 485, note. We have a still more definite account of another scholastic, Simon Tornacensis, who thought that God must feel obliged to him because he had furnished proof of the Trinity; for if he wanted to do so, he would be able to demolish that argument by stronger proofs to the contrary: *profecto si malignando et adversando vellem, fortioribus argumentis scirem illam infirmare et deprimendo improbare.* In reward for his pains the good man became a fool who had to spend two years learning his letters. Cf. Tennemann, *Geschichte der Philosophie,* Vol. 8, p. 314, note. Be that as it may, whether he actually said this or uttered the famous blasphemy of the Middle Ages about the three great deceivers [Moses, Christ and Mohammed] which also was ascribed to him, what he lacked was certainly not rigorous seriousness in the use of dialectics and speculation, but he surely lacked understanding of himself. This story has analogies enough, and in our age speculative philosophy has arrogated to itself such authority that it has almost tempted God to feel uncertain about Himself, like a king who waits anxiously to learn whether the Constitutional Assembly will make him an absolute or a limited monarch.

[The Latin sayings in this note may be translated thus: "Albertus was suddenly transformed from an ass into a philosopher, and from a philosopher into an ass." Simon, after demonstrating the truth of the Trinity, was presumptuous enough to boast: "If I were spiteful and contentious enough to wish to do so, I could demolish this proof by stronger arguments, and disprove it by surpassing it."]

wardness. But the man who has not rightly understood the eternal, understood it quite concretely,* lacks inwardness and seriousness.

I do not wish to go into details here, yet I will indicate several points.

(a). Some deny the eternal in man. That very instant "the wine of life is drawn," and every such individuality is demoniacal. If one posits the eternal, the present becomes a different thing from what one would have it be. One fears this, and thus one is in dread of the good. A man may keep on denying as long as he will, he does not by this succeed in killing the eternal entirely. And even if one is willing to a certain degree and in a certain sense to admit the eternal, one is then afraid of the other sense and the other degree; but however one may deny it, one does not get rid of it altogether. In our age men fear the eternal only too much, even when they recognize it in abstract terms and use phrases which are flattering to the eternal. While nowadays the various governments are living in fear of restless leaders, there are only too many individualities which are in fear of one restless leader which nevertheless is the true rest—eternity. Then they preach the instant, and just as the path of perdition is paved with good intentions, so is eternity most easily disposed of by living merely in instants. But why are they in such terrible haste? If there is no eternity, the instant is in fact just as long as if there were. But dread of eternity makes the instant an abstraction.—Moreover, this denial of eternity may be expressed directly and indirectly in various ways, as mockery, as prosaic intoxication with common sense, as bustle, as enthusiasm for the temporal, etc.

(b). The eternal is conceived in a perfectly abstract way. Like the blue mountains the eternal is the confine of the temporal, but he who lives energetically in the temporal never gets to the confine. The particular individual who reconnoiters it is the frontier soldier who stands outside of time.

(c). Some people bend eternity back into time to please the imagination.[33] Conceived in this way it produces an enchanting effect, one does not know whether it is dream or reality; eternity peeps sadly, dreamily, roguishly, into the instant, as the beams of the moon peep tremblingly into a lighted grove or into a hall. Thought of the eternal becomes a fantastic occupation, and the mood is

---

* It was doubtless in this sense Constantine Constantius said that eternity is the true repetition.[34]

constantly this: "Am I dreaming, or is it eternity that is dreaming of me?"

Or it is conceived purely for the imagination, unmixed with this coquettish ambiguity. This conception has found a definite expression in the maxim that art is an anticipation of eternal life.[35] For poetry and art are no more than the atonement which imagination offers and may have the *Sinnigkeit* of intuition but by no manner of means the *Innigkeit* of seriousness.—Eternity is gilded with the tinsel of imagination, and one longs for it.—One gazes apocalyptically at eternity, playing at being a Dante, whereas Dante,[36] after all, however much he conceded to visions of the imagination, did not suspend the effect of the ethical verdict.

(d). Eternity is conceived metaphysically. One keeps on saying "*Ich—Ich*"[37] until one becomes this most ludicrous of all things: the pure ego, the eternal self-consciousness. One talks about immortality till one becomes oneself—not immortal, but an immortality. In spite of all this one suddenly discovers that one has not included immortality in the System, and now one is intent upon finding a place for it in an appendix. Apropos of this ludicrous device, it was a true word Poul Møller uttered[38] when he said that immortality must be present everywhere. But if this be so, then the temporal becomes something quite different from what one would wish it to be.—Or eternity is metaphysically conceived in such a way that the temporal is comically preserved in it.[39] As seen from a purely aesthetic-metaphysical standpoint the temporal is always comic, for it is contradiction, and the comical always comes under this category. If one conceives eternity in a purely metaphysical way, and in spite of that would for some reason or another like to get the temporal included in it, it then becomes comical enough that an immortal spirit [like Mephistopheles] conserves a remembrance that several times he was in pecuniary embarrassment, etc. But all the trouble one takes in this instance to uphold immortality is labor lost and a false alarm, for no man becomes immortal, and no man becomes convinced of his immortality, in a purely metaphysical way. But if a man becomes convinced of it in quite another way, the comical will not intrude itself upon him. Even though Christianity teaches that at the Day of Judgment a man must give account of every idle word he has spoken, which we understand simply as a total recollection, of which unmistakable symptoms are occasionally to be found already in this life, and even though the doctrine of Christianity cannot be more sharply illuminated by any contrast than it is by the Greek conception that the immortal souls first drank of Lethe in order to forget,[40] yet it does not by any means follow that recollection must either directly or indirectly become comic, directly by the fact that one remembers ludicrous incidents, indirectly by transforming ludicrous incidents into essential decisions. Precisely because the accounting and the judgment are the essential concern, this essential will have the effect of the water of Lethe so far as concerns the unessential, while it also is true that many things will prove to be essential which one hardly thought to be such. In the drolleries of life, its chance happenings, its folderols, the soul has not been essentially present, and hence all this vanishes, except for the soul which was essentially in this, yet for that soul it will hardly have comic significance. When one has reflected thoroughly upon the comical, has studied it with determination, constantly keeping its category clear, one will easily understand that the comical belongs precisely to the temporal, for it is there we find contradiction. Metaphysically and aesthetically one cannot stop it and prevent it from devouring the whole of the temporal, which will happen to one who is developed enough to use the comical but not mature enough to distinguish *inter et inter*. In eternity, on the other hand, all contradiction is eliminated, the temporal is permeated by and conserved in the eternal; but here there is no trace of the comical.

But men are not willing to think eternity seriously, they dread it, and dread discovers a hundred ways of escape. But this precisely is the demoniacal.

CHAPTER V

Dread as a Saving Experience
by Means of Faith

In one of Grimm's Fairy Tales[1] there is the story of a youth who went out in search of adventures for the sake of learning what it is to fear or be in dread. We will let that adventurer go his way without troubling ourselves to learn whether in the course of it he encountered the dreadful. On the other hand I would say that learning to know dread is an adventure which every man has to affront if he would not go to perdition either by not having known dread or by sinking under it. He therefore who has learned rightly to be in dread has learned the most important thing.

If a man were a beast or an angel, he would not be able to be in dread. Since he is a synthesis he can be in dread, and the greater the dread, the greater the man. This, however, is not affirmed in the sense in which men commonly understand dread, as related to something outside a man, but in the sense that man himself produces dread. Only in this sense can we interpret the passage where it is said of Christ that he was in dread [*ængstes*] even unto death, and the place also where he says to Judas, "What thou doest, do quickly." Not even the terrible word upon which even Luther dreaded to preach, "My God, my God, why hast thou forsaken me?"—not even this expresses suffering so strongly. For this word indicates a situation in which Christ actually is; the former sayings indicate a relation to a situation which is not yet actual.

Dread is the possibility of freedom. Only this dread is by the aid of faith absolutely educative, consuming as it does all finite aims and discovering all their deceptions. And no Grand Inquisitor has in readiness such terrible tortures as has dread, and no spy knows how to attack more artfully the man he suspects, choosing the instant when he is weakest, nor knows how to lay traps where he will be caught and ensnared, as dread knows how, and no sharp-witted judge knows how to interrogate, to examine the accused, as dread does, which never lets him escape, neither by diversion nor by noise, neither at work nor at play, neither by day nor by night.

He who is educated by dread is educated by possibility, and only the man who is educated by possibility is educated in accordance with his infinity. Possibility is therefore the heaviest of all categories. One often hears, it is true, the opposite affirmed, that possibility is so light but reality is heavy. But from whom does one hear such talk? From a lot of miserable men who never have known what possibility is, and who, since reality showed them that they were not fit for anything and never would be, mendaciously bedizened a possibility which was so beautiful, so enchanting; and the only foundation of this possibility was a little youthful tomfoolery of which they might rather have been ashamed. Therefore by this possibility which is said to be light one commonly understands the possibility of luck, good fortune, etc. But this is not possibility, it is a mendacious invention which human depravity falsely embellishes in order to have reason to complain of life, of providence, and as a pretext for being self-important. No, in possibility everything is possible, and he who truly was brought up by possibility has comprehended the dreadful as well as the smiling. When such a person, therefore, goes out from the school of possibility, and knows more thoroughly than a child knows the alphabet that he can demand of life absolutely nothing, and that terror, perdition, annihilation, dwell next door to every man, and has learned the profitable lesson that every dread which alarms [ængste] may the next instant become a fact, he will then interpret reality differently, he will extol reality, and even when it rests upon him heavily he will remember that after all it is far, far lighter than the possibility was. Only thus can possibility educate; for finiteness and the finite relationships in which the individual is assigned a place, whether it be small and commonplace or world-historical, educate only finitely, and one can always talk them around, always make something a little different out of them, always chaffer, always escape a little way from them, always keep a little apart, always prevent oneself from learning absolutely from them; and if one is to learn absolutely, the individual must in turn have the possibility in himself and himself fashion that from which he is to learn, even though the next instant it does not recognize that it was fashioned by him, but absolutely takes the power from him.

But in order that the individual may thus absolutely and infinitely be educated by possibility, he must be honest towards possibility and must have faith. By faith I mean what Hegel in his fashion calls very rightly "the inward certainty which anticipates infinity." When the discoveries of possibility are honestly administered, possibility will then disclose all finitudes but idealize them in the form of infinity, and by dread overwhelm the individual, until he in turn conquers them by the anticipation of faith.

What I say here appears perhaps to many an obscure and foolish saying, since they even boast of never having been in dread. To this I would reply that doubtless one should not be in dread of men, of finite things, but that only the man who has gone through the dread of possibility is educated to have no dread—not because he avoids the dreadful things of life, but because they always are weak in comparison with those of possibility. If on the other hand the speaker means that the great thing about him is that he has never been in dread, then I shall gladly initiate him into my explanation, that this comes from the fact that he is spirit-less.

If the individual cheats the possibility by which he is to be educated, he never reaches faith; his faith remains the shrewdness of finitude, as his school was that of finitude. But men cheat possibility in every way—if they did not, one has only to stick one's head out of the window, and one would see enough for possibility to begin its exercises forthwith. There is an engraving by Chodowiecki² which represents the surrender of Calais as viewed by the four temperaments, and the theme of the artist was to let the various impressions appear mirrored in the faces which express the various temperaments. The most commonplace life has events enough, no doubt, but the question is about possibility in the individual who is honest with himself. It is recounted of an Indian hermit who for two years had lived upon dew, that he came once to the city, tasted wine, and then became addicted to drink. This story, like every other of the sort, can be understood in many ways, one can make it comic, one can make it tragic; but the man who is educated by possibility has more than enough to occupy him in such a story. Instantly he is absolutely identified with that unfortunate man, he knows no finite evasion by which he might escape. Now the dread of possibility holds him as its prey, until it can deliver him saved into the hands of faith. In no other place does he find repose, for every other point of rest is mere nonsense, even though in men's eyes it is shrewdness. This is the reason why possibility is so absolutely educative. No man has ever become so unfortunate in reality that there was not some little residue left to him, and, as common sense observes quite truly, if a man is canny, he will find a way. But he who went through the curriculum of misfortune offered by possibility lost everything, absolutely everything, in a way that no one has lost it in reality. If in this situation he did not behave falsely towards possibility, if he did not attempt to talk around the dread which would save him, then he received everything back again, as in reality no one ever did even if he received everything tenfold, for the pupil of possibility received infinity, whereas the soul of the other expired in the finite. No one ever sank so deep in reality that he could not sink deeper, or that there might not be one or another sunk deeper than he. But he who sank in the possibility has an eye too dizzy to see the measuring rod which Tom, Dick, and Harry hold out as a straw to the drowning man; his ear is closed so that he cannot hear what the market price for men is in his day, cannot hear that he is just as good as most of them. He sank absolutely, but then in turn he floated up from the depth of the abyss, lighter now than all that is oppressive and dreadful in life. Only I do not deny that he who is educated by possibility is exposed—not to the danger of bad company and dissoluteness of various sorts, as are those who are educated by the finite, but—to one danger of downfall, and that is self-slaughter. If at the beginning of his education he misunderstands the anguish of dread, so that it does not lead him to faith but away from faith, then he is lost. On the other hand, he who is educated by possibility remains with dread, does not allow himself to be deceived by its countless counterfeits, he recalls the past precisely; then at last the attacks of dread, though they are fearful, are not such that he flees from them. For him dread becomes a serviceable spirit which against its will leads him whither he would go. Then when it announces itself, when it craftily insinuates that it has invented a new instrument of torture far more terrible than anything employed before, he does not recoil, still less does he attempt to hold it off with clamor and noise, but he bids it welcome, he hails it solemnly, as Socrates solemnly flourished the poisoned goblet, he shuts himself up with it, he says, as a patient says to the surgeon when a painful operation is about to begin, "Now I am ready." Then dread enters into his soul and searches it thoroughly, constraining out of him all the finite and the petty, and leading him hence whither he would go.

When one or another extraordinary event occurs in life, when a world-historical hero gathers heroes about him and accomplishes heroic feats, when a crisis occurs and everything becomes significant, then men wish to be in it, for these are things which educate. Quite possibly. But there is a much simpler way of being educated much more fundamentally. Take the pupil of possibility, set him in the midst of the Jutland heath where nothing happens, where the greatest event is that a partridge flies up noisily, and he experiences everything more perfectly, more precisely, more profoundly, than the man who was applauded upon the stage of universal history, in case he was not educated by possibility.

Then when the individual is by possibility educated up to faith, dread will eradicate what it has itself produced. Dread discovers fate, but when the individual would put his confidence in fate, dread turns about and takes fate away; for fate is like dread, and dread is like possibility . . . a witch's letter.[3] If the individuality is not by itself transformed with relation to fate, it will always retain a dialectical remnant, which no finitude can eradicate, any more than a man will lose faith in the lottery who does not lose it by his own act but is supposed to lose it for the fact that he constantly loses what he gambles. Even in relation to the most trifling things dread is promptly at hand so soon as the individual would sneak away from something, would expect something by chance. In itself it is a trifle, and externally, the individual can learn nothing about it from the finite, but to cut the process short dread instantly plays the trump of infinity, that of the category, and the individuality cannot take the trick. Such an individual cannot possibly fear fate in an outward sense, its changeableness and its rebuffs, for in him dread has already fashioned fate and taken away from him everything that any fate could take away. Socrates says in the dialogue of *Cratylus*[4] that it is dreadful to be deceived by oneself, because one always has the deceiver with one. So one can say that it is good fortune to have with one such a deceiver as dread, which deceives piously and weans the child before finiteness begins to bungle it. Even if in our time an individuality is not thus educated by possibility, our age has after all a characteristic which is notably helpful to one who has a deeper nature and desires to learn the good. The more peaceful and quiet an age is, the more precisely everything follows its regular course, so that the good has its reward, all the more easily can an individual be deceived with regard to the question whether the goal of its striving, though it be a beautiful one, may not be a finite goal. In these times, on the contrary, one need not be more than sixteen years of age to perceive that he who now has to tread the stage of life is pretty much in the same fix as the man who went down to Jericho and fell among thieves. He then who does not wish to sink in the wretchedness of the finite is constrained, in the deepest sense, to assault the infinite. Such a preliminary orientation is analogous to education in possibility, and such an orientation cannot possibly come about except by the help of possibility. So when shrewdness has marshalled its innumerable calculations, upon the assumption of winning the game—then comes dread, even before the game was in reality lost or won, and against the devil dread makes the sign of the cross, then there is nothing shrewdness can do, and all its most sagacious combinations vanish like a ghost before that figure which dread fashions by the omnipotence of possibility. Even in relation to the most trifling matters, so soon as the individuality would make an artful turn which is only artful, would steal away from something, and there is every probability that it will succeed, for reality is not so sharp an examiner as dread—then dread is at hand. If it is sent away on the plea that this is a trifle, then dread makes this trifle as notable as the village of Marengo became in the history of Europe, because there the great Battle of Marengo was fought. In case an individuality is not thus weaned away from shrewdness by its own act, then this is never thoroughly accomplished, for finitude explains only piece-meal, never totally, and the man whose shrewdness was always at fault (and even this is inconceivable in reality) may seek the reason for his failure in a lack of shrewdness and strive to become all the shrewder. With the help of faith dread trains the individual to find repose in providence. So also it is with regard to guilt, which is the second thing dread discovers. The man who merely by finiteness learns to recognize his guilt is lost in finiteness, and in the end the question whether one is guilty or not cannot be decided except in an external, juridical, exceedingly imperfect way. He therefore who only learns to recognize his guilt by analogy with the decisions of the police justice or the supreme court never really comprehends that he is guilty; for if a man is guilty, he is infinitely guilty. Therefore if such an individual who is educated only by finiteness does not get a verdict from the police or a verdict of public opinion that he is guilty, he becomes about the most ludicrous and pitiable of all men, a paragon of virtue who is a little better than people generally are, but not quite so good as the parson. What help does such a man need in life? Why, even before he is dead he can almost take his place in a gallery of wax figures. From finiteness one can learn much, but one cannot learn dread, except in a very mediocre and depraved sense. On the other hand, he who truly has learned to be in dread will tread as in a dance when the dreads of finiteness strike up their tune, and the disciples of finiteness lose their wits and their courage. Thus it is life often deceives. The hypochondriac is in dread of every unimportant symptom, but when the important test comes he begins to draw a full breath. And why is this? Because the important reality is not so dreadful as the possibility he himself had fashioned and employed his whole strength in fashioning, whereas now he can employ all his strength against reality. The hypochondriac, however, is only an imperfect autodidact in comparison with the man who is educated by possibility, because hypochondria depends in part upon the bodily state and therefore is fortuitous.* The true autodidact is precisely in the same degree a theodidact, as another author has said.† Or to avoid terms which stress so much the intellectual side, it may be said that he is αὐτουργός τις τῆς φιλοσοφίας ‡ and in the same degree θεουργός. He who with respect to guilt is educated by dread will therefore repose only in atonement.

Here this deliberation ends where it began. So soon as psychology has finished with dread, it has nothing to do but to deliver it over to dogmatics.

* It is therefore in a higher significance Hamann[5] employs the word "hypochondria" when he says: *Diese Angst in der Welt ist aber der einzige Beweis unserer Heterogeneität. Denn fehlte uns nichts, so würden wir es nicht besser machen als die Heiden und Transcendental-Philosophen, die von Gott nichts wissen und in die liebe Natur sich wie die Narren vergaffen; kein Heimweh würde uns anwandeln. Diese impertinente Unruhe, diese heilige Hypochondrie, ist vielleicht das Feuer, womit wir Opferthiere gesalzen und vor der Fäulniss des laufenden seculi bewahrt werden müssen.* Vol. 6, p. 194.

[Translation: "However, this dread which we experience in the world is the only proof of our heterogeneity. For if we lacked nothing, we should do no better than the pagans and the transcendental philosophers who know nothing of God and like fools fall in love with this precious world; no homesickness would attack us. This impertinent uneasiness, this holy hypochondria, is perhaps the fire whereby we sacrificial animals must be salted and preserved from the decay of the passing age." Cf. the Journal, III A 235.]

† Cf. *Either/Or.* [II, p. 226]

‡ Cf. Xenophon's *Symposium* [1, 5], where Socrates applies this word to himself.[6]

NOTES

These notes will not all of them be interesting to all readers, yet they will be useful to some, and seeing that in the course of many years they have been contributed from many quarters to the Danish editors of S.K.'s Works, they should be preserved also in the English edition.

PREFACE

¹ A grandiloquent boast made on behalf of Martensen by the man who translated into Danish M's licentiate's disputation, *De autonomia conscientiae sui humanae*, published in 1841.

² A reference to J. L. Heiberg's *Urania* which he published as a New Year's gift-book. Cf. S. K.'s *Forord* III.

³ See Holberg's *Erasmus Montanus*, act iii, scene 3.

⁴ The burghers presided in turn, a month at a time.

⁵ Meaning the watchman of Copenhagen. The Danish name, Kjøbenhavn, means "market harbor"—hence Haufniensis was used as the Latin equivalent.

INTRODUCTION

¹ Refers to Hegel's *Logik*, in which, however, it is not the last section but the last section of the middle part which has this heading.

² We learn from the *Papers* (V B 49, 2) that he had in mind Rasmus Neilsen's *De speculativo sacrae historiae tractandae methodo*, p. 6, and p. 2 of Martensen's disputation mentioned above.

³ That is, Hegel's logic (cf. *Werke* III, pp. 59 ff.). The Greek phrase above means "initial error."

⁴ Refers perhaps to Stilling's *Philosophical considerations touching the significance of speculative logic* (Copenhagen, 1842), pp. 45 f.

⁵ Hegel's *Logik*, Introduction and Conclusion (*Werke* III, pp. 40 ff., and V, pp. 329 ff.), and his *Encyclopädie*, §383. About his opposition to Kant, see especially III, p. 44.

⁶ E.g. in *System des transcendentalen Idealismus* (*Werke*, Part One, III, pp. 369 ff.).

⁷ A reference especially to Stilling's work above mentioned, p. 11. Cf. also Marheineke's *Dogmatik* (2nd ed.), §208.

⁸ Hegel's *Logik*, III (*Werke* V, p. 340) where, however, this precise expression does not occur.

⁹ Hegel, *Philosophie des Rechts*, §18, §139 *Zusatz*.

¹⁰ In *De l'Allemagne* she is reported to have said this about speculative philosophy in general, without mentioning Schelling.

¹¹ I remark once for all that by "the System" S. K. always means the Hegelian system.

¹² In Phaedrus' *Fables*, No. V, it was not the "shadow" but the reflection of meat in the water which the dog preferred.

¹³ Plato's *Gorgias*.

¹⁴ Gal. 3:24.

¹⁵ In the first draft the word καλοκαγαθια was added to express the Greek ideal of human excellence. *Kalos* = beautiful; *agathos* = good.

¹⁶ In his *Kritik des Urtheilskraft*, §2 ff.

¹⁷ He has in mind Heiberg's *Urania* mentioned before, which offended him by an appreciation of *Repetition* which totally failed to understand the point of it. He proudly resolved not to reply in print, but he wrote a long answer which

the *Papers*, from which I quoted something in my Preface to
rs IV B 101-124.
us redivivus by Hase, §73 ff., §38 ff.
*emocritus, but also some earlier philosophers, such as Anaxi-

----

[20] Schleiermacher's *Christliche Glaube* (Berlin, 1821-22).

[21] In his *Metaphysics* (V 1) Aristotle called the "first philosophy" also the "theological."

[22] In his Berlin lectures, which S. K. heard, but which in 1844 were not yet published (*Werke*, Part Two, III, p. 103). Cf. *Papers* IV C 46.

[23] Leibnitz, *Opera philosophica* (Erdmann's ed., 1840), p. 78.

[24] "Do not disturb my circles," Archimedes is reported to have said when the soldiers interrupted him in his work and slew him (Valerius Maximus, viii, 7, *Ext. 7*).

[25] Hegel, *Encyclopädie* §387; Rosenkrantz, *Psychologie oder der Wissenschaft vom subjectiven Geist* (Königsberg, 1837).

CHAPTER I

[1] Affirmed (though not precisely in these terms) in the *Catechismus Romanus*, I, 2, 19, and in *Hutterus redivivus*, §80, 4, §81: the supernatural and wonderful gift of divinity.

[2] A school of theology which had its origin in Holland in the 17th century. Cf. Bretschneider's *Dogmatik* (3rd ed.) I, p. 68, II, p. 70 f.

[3] The Danish editors affirm that neither of these positions was rejected by Protestantism: the first they find in *Formula Concordiae* II, 1, 10 (cp. *Apologia Augustanae Confessionis* II, 15-23); the latter in *Apol. Aug. Conf.* II, 38 and II, 47.

[4] The first two being common Lutheran definitions, the last peculiar to the Covenant theology: The head of the human race by nature, by generation, by Covenant.

[5] *Darstellung meines Systems*, §23 ff.

[6] *Principia quaedam disciplinae naturali, in primis chemiae, ex metaphysica naturale substernenda* (Tübingen, 1796), Cf. Schelling's consonant ideas upon natural philosophy (*Werke* I, *Abth.* II, p. 313).

[7] *Logik*, I (*Werke* III), pp. 402 ff., 450.

[8] *Psychologie* (2nd ed.), p. 352.

[9] A figure in Holberg's play, *The Reviewer and the Beast*, who boasted that any instant he could get a testimonial that he *almost* passed his law examination.

[10] But for this St. Paul was responsible: Rom. 5:12-21; I Cor. 15:21 f.

[11] The wards of an orphan asylum in Copenhagen who were so called because they were dressed uniformly in blue. The boys addressed each other by their numbers instead of by name.

[12] E.g. Marheineke's *Dogmatik*, §260.

[13] *Logik*, I, pp. 110 f.; III, p. 340.

[14] *Logik*, I, p. 78.

[15] *Entwickelung des paulinischen Lehrbegriffes* (4th ed., Zürich, 1832), I Theil, 2 Abschn., pp. 28 ff.

[16] *Vorlesungen über religiöse Philosophie*, §35 (*Werke* I, pp. 249 ff.).

[17] Cambyses, who according to Polyaen, *Strategemata* 7, 9, placed animals sacred to the Egyptians in front of his army when he was besieging Pelusium. For fear of hitting them, the Egyptians ceased fire, and the victory was won.

[18] *Conf. Aug.* I, 2, 1: "All men begotten in a natural way are born with sin, i.e. without the fear of God, without trust in God, and with concupiscence."

[19] "My other" is my eternal life or spirit. It is in the state of innocency that the spirit, as in a dream, manifests itself as possibility. That is, one senses freedom.

[20] From the context, what one expects is "possibility for freedom," and the Danish editors do not hesitate to say that this is what is meant. To establish their point, they refer to p. 81 where we read that "the possibility of freedom manifests itself before freedom" and to p. 99 where it is recalled that dread has been defined as "freedom's appearance before itself in possibility." In *Sickness unto Death* S. K. uses "possibility" and "freedom" interchangeably.

[21] Such queries as St. Augustine raises in *De Civitate Dei* (14, 23) as to whether there would have been procreation in paradise if there had been no sin.

[22] He got this expression from Leibnitz. Cf. *Papers* IV C 31, 36, 39.

[23] In Grimm's *Fairy Tales* (*Kinder- und Hausmärchen*, No. 34).

[24] *Very* round numbers. 4004 B.C. is of course the traditional date of the Creation. Nebuchadnezzar lived about 600 B.C.

[25] A bookseller in Copenhagen who was notorious for his absent-mindedness.

CHAPTER II

[1] Rom. 8:19.

[2] Chapter IV, §2.

[3] E.g. in *Speculative Dogmatik*, XVII (*Werke* VII, pp. 143 ff.).

[4] The first draft mentions Schubert, Eschenmayer, Görres, Steffens.

[5] E.g. in *Logik*, I, p. 43; with express reference to the Platonic expression, τὸ ἕτερον, *Geschichte der Philosophie*, II (*Werke*, XIV, [2nd ed.], p. 213).

[6] *Philosophische Untersuchungen über das Wesen der menschlichen Freiheit* (*Werke* I, Abth. VII, p. 399).

[7] *Zur Kritik der Schellingschen Offenbarungsphilosophie* (Berlin 1843), p. 47.

[8] It is evident from the first draft that S.K. had consulted Rosenkrantz's *Schelling*, in which this expression is used.

[9] *Erasmus Montanus*, act iv, scene 4.

[10] Refers doubtless to the *Memorabilia*, 2, 6, 32, although there Socrates proposes that ugly young men might be kissed to cheer them with the thought that they were loved for their beautiful souls.

[11] Xenophon's *Memorabilia*, 1, 3, 8 ff.

[12] "Our [Belgian] maidens do not know that in the glance of the eye and in the kiss there is an introduction to lust, therefore they use them. Yours [i.e. the Italian maidens] know it." Bayle's *Lexicon, sub* "Puteanus," note J.

[13] *Dipnosophia*, 5 B, p. 219 d.

[14] Plutarch's *Pericles*, 24, 2.

[15] *Symposium*, 2, 10.

[16] The name bestowed in those days upon an animal which puzzled naturalists, since it began like a frog and ended as a fish.

[17] Beginning with Kant's *Religion innerhalb der Grenzen der blossen Vernunft*, I, section iii. Cf. Hegel's *Philosophie des Rechts*, §139, and *Philosophie der Religion*, II (*Werke* XII [2nd ed.], 2).

[18] In Grundtvig's *Nordens Mythologi* (2nd ed., 1832), on p. 413, it is said the "myth-smiths" possessed a "falcon-eye" for the course of human history. "Jew's-harp" is a favorite word of Grundtvig's.

[19] This may be aimed at Stilling: *Philosophical considerations about speculative logic*, p. 12.

[20] According to Hase's *Hutterus redivivus*, §130, 7, the sexual difference is preserved in the resurrection, but *excluso semine et lacte*.

[21] See Bretschneider's *Dogmatik* (3rd ed.), I, §101, 2. (Cf. Luke 20:34-36).

[22] "Cheerfulness." Hegel, *Philosophie der Religion*, II, p. 131.

CHAPTER III

[1] The name which describes certain Greek monks who, like the Buddhists, gazed at the navel as an aid to profound meditation.

[2] Cf. *Papers* IV B I, p. 143; V B 55, 3.

[3] The *Dyrehaven* is a vast park surrounded by forests at a considerable distance from Copenhagen, to which the citizens commonly resorted on holidays.

[4] "Coffee-mill" was the disparaging name bestowed upon this popular means of conveyance.

[5] See Hegel, *Philosophie der Geschichte* (*Werke* IX [2nd ed.], p. 200).

[6] She figures in Tegnér's *Frithiofs Saga* IX, but here it evidently is a picture S. K. has in mind.

[7] In his *Phaedo* Plato draws a proof of the immortality of the soul from the fact that in this life we have conceptions, such as the good and the beautiful, which can only be explained as recollections of a previous existence.

[8] In the *Phaedo* Plato recommends to the philosopher the ascetic discipline of dying from the sensible world, a thought which is prominent also in the New Testament—and not merely in ascetic theology.

[9] It appears from *Papers* V B 56, 7, that S. K. had in mind "the Ancient of Days" in Daniel 7 :9, 13, 22.

[10] *Wie die Alten den Tod gebildet* (*Werke* VIII [Maltzahn's ed.], pp. 197-248).

[11] Socrates and Hamann. Cf. the motto of this book on the back of the title page.

[12] In Matt. 5 :13 and Luke 14 :34 the word $\mu\omega\rho\alpha\nu\theta\hat{\eta}$, which we translate "lost its savor" is derived from $\mu\omega\rho\acute{o}s$, which means "stupid," "foolish." Hence, moron.

[13] Cf. Hegel's *Aesthetik* (*Werke* X, Part One, pp. 364 f.).

[14] *An sich* is a term Hegel uses to denote that something is *for* itself alone, not "for another." See *Logik*, pp. 125 ff. As applied to genius it means that, irreligiously, it has its aim and its law within itself, not outside itself.

[15] Plutarch, *Caesar*, 38.

[16] A sect of Gnostics in the 2nd century who taught that one must taste all human experience, even all vices, on the way to perfection. This notion, as we see from the Journal, fascinated S. K.

[17] He means the monastic life, which also fascinated him with a sympathetic antipathy which compelled him to return to the thought again and again. The Journal shows that in his later years the sympathy predominated.

[18] In the *Protagoras*.

[19] "Love of Fame," II, 208.

CHAPTER IV

[1] E.g. *Theodoce*, §319 f. Cf. *Papers* IV C 39.

[2] All these expressions amount to the same thing : lazy reasoning. It was thus that Chrysippus, and afterwards Cicero (*De fato*, 12, 28), characterized the fatalistic view. S. K. gets these terms from Leibnitz, *Theodoce*, §55. Cf. *Papers* IV A 12.

[3] In Kruse's rendering of *Don Juan*, act ii, last scene.

[4] Does in fact in his *System des Transcendentalen Idealismus*, *Werke* I, *Abth.* III, p. 549.

[5] Act iv, scene 6. "Masterpiece" is one of the improvements of the German translator.

[6] Railroads and the telegraph being new in his day, S. K. constantly referred to them as wonders.

[7] Among other places in *Die Bestimmung des Menschen*, *Werke* II, p. 311.

[8] *Physiognomische Fragmente* (Leipzig 1775-78).

[9] The phrase "to have made studies" exactly describes S. K.'s own case; for in his university years he had spent a prodigious amount of time studying the darker aspects of the Middle Ages, proposing to write a book on Faust, Don Juan, and the Wandering Jew, illustrating the themes of doubt, sensuality, and despair.

[10] Not quite the punishment of death, it seems, for in his "Letter to Donatus" he reprobates this notion, which Tertullian, however, recommends in *Scorpiace* 2.

[11] *Gorgias.*

[12] I.e., the Danish word *Indesluttedhed*, for which, alas, we have no equivalent in English. "Concludedness" is a word that has been suggested to me because etymologically it *might* have this meaning; but the reader will perceive that it would not fit here in every instance, perhaps in none. In translating other works of S. K. where this word occurs less frequently, I have been accustomed to use "close reserve," also "morbid reserve," even "introversion"; but here where this concept is the principal theme and is illuminated from every side I could not be so easygoing. But it is a dreadful alternative to have to say "shut-upness." At this point, having plagued the reader long enough with this word, and having got beyond the passage where *Indesluttedhed* is carefully defined, I feel free to return to "close reserve." The German translator is in no difficulty, for he has the word *Verschlossenheit*. Of the French translators, M. Gateau uses the term *hermétisme* commonly, but also *taciturne* and *réservé*, whereas M. Tisseau employs at least a dozen words: *l'esprit renfermé, repliement de l'esprit, mutisme*, and I cannot recall what all.

[13] I.e., communicating in the Sacrament of the Lord's Supper.

[14] Mark 5:7. We translate it, "What have I to do with thee?" Cp. Luke 8:28.

[15] In Mark 5:17 the people of Gedara beseech Christ to depart from their coasts, but there seems to be no reference in the Gospels to a demoniac's having besought Christ to go another way.

[16] Yes indeed! And S. K. was the most notable example of it. This book is pseudonymous, and what follows here is the most intimate self-revelation.

[17] Act i, scene 2.

[18] He acted this part from 1827 to 1834, the year of his death; *The Inseparables* is a play by Heiberg.

[19] A celebrated Swedish song-writer.

[20] In a review of Solger's posthumous papers, *Werke* XVI, p. 487.

[21] *Philosophische Untersuchungen über das Wesen der menschlichen Freiheit, Werke I, Abth.* VII, p. 387.

[22] See note 14 above.

[23] Cf. Stilling, *Philosophical Considerations, etc.*, pp. 34, 37.

[24] *Ueber den Begriff der Wissenschaftslehre, Werke* I, pp. 40 ff.

[25] A word invented by S. K. In the *Stages*, p. 340, he wrote the word in Greek, and I translated it by "strikingly appropriate." Literally it means "pointing out," "indicative." Here it means the personal application.

[26] *Die christliche Mystik*, in 4 vols. (1836).

[27] *Macbeth*, act ii, scene 3.

[28] *Pars* I, *Artic.* LIII.

[29] In *Theaetetus* Plato says: "For this state of wonder is characteristic precisely of the philosopher, for there is no other beginning of philosophy but this." In the *Metaphysics* I, 2, Aristotle says: "For because they wondered men began to philosophize, and began this only then." S. K. insists that wonder is the beginning of religion. See especially the fragment I print as an appendix to the *Stages*, pp. 457 ff., but also *Christian Discourses*, pp. 111 ff.

[30] *Metaphysics*, II, §201-04.

[31] *Psychologie* (1st ed., 1837). *Gemüth* means the characteristic temper of the soul. I can do no better here than to translate it by "temperament." So the passage would read: "[it is essential] that the feeling open itself to consciousness, and inversely that the content of consciousness be felt by the subject as *his own.* Only this unity can be called temperament. For if clarity of recognition is lacking, that is, a knowledge of the feeling, there exists only the urge of natural impulse, the turgidity of immediacy. If, however, the feeling is lacking, there exists only an abstract concept which has not attained the intensity of spiritual being, has not become one with the self of the spirit." In the next passage I translate *Seelenhaftigkeit* by "soulishness"—perhaps because I have a fondness for this word. "Feeling" then is said to be the spirit's "immediate unity of its soulishness and its consciousness." I confess that all this means very little to me.

[32] No, it is in his chapter on "Anthropology," Part Second, chapter 3.

[33] S. K.'s first notes for this book (V B 60, p. 137; and 72, 32) show that he was thinking here of the *Letters of Bettina von Arnim.*

[34] It was the young man, however, who said this, not Constantine; cf. *supra* p. 17.

[35] "Art is an anticipation of the blessed life" said Poul Møller in his *Efterladte Skrifter* (2nd ed.), p. 90.

[36] Aiming at Heiberg's *A Soul After Death*, and Martensen's review of it in the *Fatherland*, 1841. Cf. *Papers* IV B 46 (p. 203).

[37] A favorite term of the idealistic philosophy, which was first used by Fichte, then by Schelling and Hegel, to denote, first the empirical "I," then the absolute "I" which is identical with "the Absolute."

[38] In his *Treatise on Immortality*, IV (*Vaerker* V [2nd ed.], pp. 65-76), where he calls attention to the embarrassment of the Hegelians in dealing with personal immortality, and remarks that no place was found for it in the System.

[39] A reference to Martensen's review which was mentioned above in note 36; cp. *Papers* V B 60, p. 137, where S. K. also refers to Hegel's *Aesthetik.*

[40] This notion is found first in Plato's *Republic*, X, 621c.

CHAPTER V

[1] *Kinder- und Hausmärchen*, I, No. 4; II, No. 121.

[2] In 1762 a guiltless Jean Calas was executed. Presently Voltaire took a hand in the matter, and the judge was dismissed. In 1767 Chodowiecki made an engraving which profoundly caught the imagination of his contemporaries: "In Prison Calas takes leave of his Family before the Execution." Later Chodowiecki, in another drawing, portrayed four persons, symbolizing the four temperaments, beholding "Les Adieux de Calas." For reasons too involved and too unimportant to explain here, S. K. has confused the farewell of Calas with "the surrender of Calais."

[3] A witch's letter (*Heksebrev*) is a book containing a number of pictures, cut in two, of men or animals. The top halves and the bottom halves can be united in many different combinations to form all manner of strange figures.

[4] Cf. *Papers* IV A 124.

[5] Cf. *Papers* III A 235.

[6] A "self-taught man in philosophy," in contrast to one who has learned it from others; αὐτουργός is properly used of a farmer who cultivates his own land himself. From the context, θεουργός must then mean one who works in the service of God.

INDEX

For the significance of "dread" when associated with "good," "evil," "innocence," "consciousness," "sin," "the first sin," "original sin," "the Fall," "guilt," "fate," "faith," and according as it is objective or subjective, consult the Table of Contents on p. 7.